REFLECTIONS *from* *a* ROMAN LAKE

On the front cover

The watercolor on the cover showing Trevignano Romano is by Elizabeth Campell, painted in 1825. A native of Argyllshire, Scotland, she traveled widely and painted in France, Switzerland and Italy between 1819 and 1827. Miss Campbell was among the many British artists to travel to the Continent when the Grand Tour was revived following the end of the Napleonic Wars; the most famous of those recording the Grand Tour sites was J.W. Turner, whose sketchbooks are in the Tate Museum, London.

Besides Trevignano, in Central Italy Miss Campbell painted Bracciano with its castle, the towns of Isola Farnese and Nepi, and idyllic scenes of the Campagna Romana countryside.

Her brother was Sir Neil Campbell, an officer in the British Army, who escorted Napoleon to his first exile on the isle of Elba in 1814 and was later appointed Governor General of the African colony of Sierra Leone, where he died in 1827.

On the back cover
Photograph by Giampiero Marricchi.

Contents

1

Black Swans

Blessed is the tree
that drapes itself in its own leaves

Bracciano proverb[1]

The four black swans arrived at nightfall a few years ago. Over the decades the pure white swans seen from the lake shore town of Trevignano Romano had expanded into a flock of twenty-five or so, but never had we seen their black brethren. Sharp of eye and slightly frightening, they sported blood-red beaks with white tips. By comparison with the sturdy bodies of the white swans, these newcomers appeared thinner and agile enough to fly over fences. Whose fences, from where? We would never know.

The swans make their home on Lake Bracciano, which lies 25 miles or so north of Rome. For the ancient Romans this was Lacus Sabatinus, named after the god "Sabazios." From ancient Thrace (modern Bulgaria) the cult of Sabazios spread throughout Greece and then to the Roman empire and all the way to Lake Bracciano, where he gave the name to its ancient Roman town of Sabate; the name survives in today's Anguillara Sabazia, one of the lake's three towns.

So who was he? Like his Greek counterpart Dionysus and his Roman equivalent Bacchus, Sabazios represented wine and ritual ecstasy (with a hint of madness) and, especially, fertility. The upper-crust ancient Roman male had little use for this sort of thing: he honored the more proper gods by strutting through town in show-off daytime processions. Covering his face, he would hold on a stick a wax effigy of an illustrious forebear.

By contrast, the wilder cults of Sabazios and Dionysus/Bacchus were celebrated by night by women and slaves. Adorned in garlands woven of grape leaves and ivy, the women, in defiance of their husbands, would dance to the music of pipes and drums by torchlight in the fields. In the iconography of Sabazios the phallus also made its appearance.

In short, Sabazios aka Dionysus/Bacchus is a legendary delight. Where else can one feed the swans in a Bacchanalian lake and then sip locally produced wine on its shore?

The white swans who thrive on the lake have their own history. They were originally brought to Lake Bracciano in the 1940s by a Swiss couple, Hildegard and her husband

Two black and four white swans witness bridal joy on Lake Bracciano, Trevignano beach.

Xavier Leutenegger, personnel director of the United Nations Food and Agriculture Organization (FAO) in Rome. While weekending on Lake Bracciano their boat capsized, and for seven hours they clung to its hull until the current carried them to the shore at the town of Anguillara. There fishermen rescued them and took them home and put them to bed. The result was their falling in love with the area and its people. They bought a home at lakeside.

It happened that Hildegard was born on the Swiss–German border by Lake Constance, which was considered overpopulated with swans. From that lake she was offered a pair of Lake Constance swans, free of charge. "On the way into Italy, passing the customs point, the guards let them wander free for a few minutes and even fed them," Leutenegger, by then in her nineties, told me as we sat in her house and gazed out over the lake. "So I put them in the lake.

"But guess what happened: the fishermen feared they would kill the fish. And then hunters came along and killed them, for food." Their being considered a food was not entirely unusual: swans had been a dining favorite of the Tudor English, including Queen Elizabeth I, who presented them served at table, baked and decorated with their own feathers. Until fairly recently they were still offered as a treat at British weddings.

Distressed, Leutenegger had new swans brought the following year, only to have hunters kill these too. But she persisted, year after year, in bringing swans to Lake Bracciano. Eventually the local hunters grasped that, however much the Tudors relished swan meat, it was not all that tasty. Finally the swans and Leutenegger prevailed. (This story was also recounted in the magazine *La Voce del Lago* in April 2003.)

One of my own joys of life is to watch these descendants of the now deceased Hildegard Leutenegger's Swiss swans dive upside down for their breakfast, displaying above water a pyramid of perpendicular white tail feathers. In the afternoon, when I first had an apartment by the lake, I would walk down to the waterfront restaurant called the Casina Bianca. The swans could tell time: around 3:30 or so they would arrive in a little fleet, their mighty wings whirring in the wind like a single celestial engine, for a takeout late lunch. When the restaurant patrons had moved on, the owner of the Casina Bianca, a hard-working Neapolitan woman, regularly seated herself at the shoreline and tossed into the water leftover crusts of bread.

And now there were black swans as well. In times past, no one even knew such a thing as a black swan existed. For millennia, literally, they were assumed to be unreal, and this unreality gave birth to myriad fanciful theories. Juvenal (AD 60–130) began it, writing sarcastically in his "On the Ways of Women,"

> Ask, "Can a worthy wife to be found among all these crowds?" One who is pretty, charming, rich and fertile, with ancient ancestors ranged about her halls, and yet more chaste than the disheveled Sabine maidens who stopped the war? T'would be a prodigy as rare upon this earth as a black swan.

His phrase deploring the scarcity of a good woman, *Rara avis in terris nigroque simillima cygno*, came to be taken as fact: as everyone knows, swans have white feathers and so black swans do not exist. By extension, in sixteenth-century London anything non-existent came to be called "a black swan."

Even in our own time, when real ones have been known to exist for a few centuries, the black swan image persists as a useful literary metaphor for events that defy normal expectations and probability. Nassim Nicholas Taleb, professor of risk engineering at New York University, gave the phrase a new lease on life in his book *The Black Swan* (2007). In it Taleb argues that people tend to be blind to the random event that "deviates beyond what is normally expected of a situation and is extremely difficult to predict."[2] Proof of his thesis was that, during the anti-European Union referendum "Brexit" vote in Great Britain in June 2016, a political commentator justified Brexit by warning of the risk that a migrant-staged terrorist attack, which he dubbed a "black swan event," could take place even at a soccer match. (In the event, the black swan turned out to be Brexit itself, of course.)

The sight of four black swans suddenly flying close to the shore of Lake Bracciano, an hour north of Rome, was a genuine black swan event. As I gaped, a fellow morning dogwalker along the waterfront remarked, in elegant Latin with an English accent, "*Cygnus atratus*. Probably escaped from a zoo. They come from Australia, you know. The cobs share the tending of the cygnets." Cobs? When I looked that up later, I learned that a "cob" is a male swan.

"How do you know all this?" I asked him.

"I am visiting from a town on the Thames, where there is already a colony of black swans. They belong to the Queen. They are quite aggressive, you know. They drive the other swans away."

However, as if to demonstrate the serendipital unpredictability that would have pleased Professor Taleb, the new black swans did not drive away their fellow winged creatures. Instead they eschewed aggressive traits to emulate the white swans, begging for bits of stale bread from the children who brought little bags of old bread down to the waterfront. Like the swans, the children had never been told that swans, white or black, are aggressive. Unsqueamish, the youngsters often fed the swans by hand. The local colony of white swans had long since learned not to bite the wee hands that fed them.

The first couple of black swans were introduced by a local Anguillara shop owner, Franco Pariciani, who had already introduced mallard and mandarin ducks and Canadian geese. The two were killed by fearful locals, but somehow other black swans survived and settled on the lake. Two eventually drifted or flew away, and were sighted in the nearby lakefront town of Anguillara Sabazia. The other two have remained, and have generated four cygnets. Together they all swim in a surprisingly congenial way amidst the white swans and the other birds gathered in watery assembly: mallards, geese, gulls, ducks, coots, herons, ibises. On the grey pebble beach nearby heedless flocks of doves, pigeons and blackbirds scrabble.

Nineteenth-century Trevignano town hall fresco: hilltop fortress ruins above Renaissance church.

Like the swans, I flew here on wings that, as it turned out, were of happiness. Trevignano Romano (its proper name) is a little town on the northern shore of Lake Bracciano. It is one of a half dozen volcanic lakes near Rome, but nowhere is summer prettier than on our lake—ours in my mind, at least, because I have now had a house overlooking that lake for over a quarter century. In summer especially the lake drapes herself in a shawl of morning calm. Evening sunsets can be gaudy-gorgeous.

From my hilltop terrace, two towns with ancient origins are visible. Looking to the right across the water is the largest and most famous, Bracciano, built around its huge historic castle of grey stone. To the left is Anguillara Sabazia. Poised high on a bluff jutting into the lake, Anguillara with its watch tower served first the ancient Romans and later medieval Rome as an outpost guarding the road toward Rome.

For foreign consumption, to describe Italian towns journalists at least used to employ words like "quaint" and "picturesque", with a hint of the patronizing. Though the words seem slightly denigrating and *vieux jeu*, our small town of Trevignano is just that: as quaint and picturesque as even the most jaded writer of travel brochures could conjure up. (I know: I've done that.) But Trevignano is far more than that. Trevignano not only has the most charm of the three lake towns, but is also the oldest. While smaller and less well known (hoorah!) than the others, and despite the spectacular castle at Bracciano, it vaunts the richest heritage.

These postcards from my personal paradise—the merest footnotes to the record of the town's deep past—aim to tell its long, long story, plus tales about a few of the people who once lived in the village, and who live there today: the eighteenth-century visionary who was the first in Italy to teach the hearing impaired to speak, the blind town crier who shouted the news through the streets, the midwife who for four decades delivered every baby born here. The gifted sculptor who collects rubbish. The photographer who learned to fly an airplane at age sixty-seven. The talented baker. The composer-director Stefano Cucci, who for twenty years oversaw the concerts performed abroad by Ennio Morricone, the world's most famous composer of movie music. The most popular of all Trevignano residents, an American who has lived in Trevignano for over six decades and recently celebrated his 108th birthday.

In Italy, the historical, geographical and cultural differences, from the Alpine arc to the islands in the south, are so acute that they have affected the language itself, to the point that the dialects in the north and south can still on occasion be mutually incomprehensible. This changed little after 1870, when a half dozen statelets were finally slapped together to form an at least formally united Italy. But separation can seem superficial: at this writing, when Venice is still popular with tourists, a campaign is underway there to revive the Venetian dialect. The differences persist, and even little Trevignano has its own dialectal phrases, as we shall see.

This is not really surprising. Throughout time, the deep past has left deep impressions upon the present. The history of Trevignano and its near neighbors can be traced in a straight line from the Stone Age through the centuries of the Etruscan culture and the Roman empire, from the Middle Ages through the Renaissance, and from Nazi occupation during the Second World War through today's gentrification and pop tourism. That history, together with the peculiar geology of the lake and a micro-climate that allows the lemon trees in our garden to bear fruit all winter, makes the town different from any other, anywhere in the world. It is unique. In fact, geology was destiny.

Trevignano has enjoyed three moments of particular glory. The first "moment," which lasted a thousand years or so, came with the ancient Romans. Pushing north to seize power in the fourth century BC, Roman soldiers built the Via Cassia, still the area's most important road. From it, cutting across country to reach the sea, they added a road that swept alongside the northern shore of the 22-square-mile Lake Bracciano. At Trevignano they rebuilt the old Etruscan fortress atop a steep hill of hardened volcanic rock.

The importance of this fortress has conditioned the town ever since. Hovering high above the lake it provided a remarkable lookout. Furthermore, directly beneath this sheer wall of solid rock passes the sole road possible, given the geology. A funnel only a handful of yards wide, this stretch of road makes any enemy extremely vulnerable—and made tiny Trevignano loom large in the defense of Rome for at least fifteen centuries.

Innocent III, the most influential pope in the Middle Ages, refortified Rome. Given the strategic importance of Trevignano, he also had the old fortress there rebuilt into a mighty castle in 1301. Embraced within its sturdy walls, which extended from hilltop castle to lake shore, was a settlement of soldiers and farmers, the *borgo*.

Two centuries later the castle was owned by the Orsini. The Borgia pope Alexander VI, who despised the Orsini, dispatched his (presumed) illegitimate son Giovanni Borgia to attack the castle at Trevignano. From a nearby hilltop, utilizing new-fangled cannon, Giovanni destroyed the castle. It never recovered, and lies in ruins today. However, sacked by Borgia's soldiers, its medieval *borgo* survived through plague and famine until today, when it remains extraordinarily popular.

The subsequent poverty meant that few new buildings were added in later centuries, and few changes made. The narrow streets within the two old *borgo* gates remain by and large as they were in the Middle Ages.

And this long sleep accounts for the town's third renaissance: becoming a favorite attraction today for Romans as well as for other Italian and foreign tourists. Becoming a tour destination, and suddenly widely publicized, has made its waterfront a cheery promenade of restaurants and cafés. Simply to hang out in one of these for people watching is among the most enchanting of occupations.

Until now, its relative isolation had enhanced Trevignano's individuality and fostered a certain toughness among the locals plus the successful conservation of its culture. And in fact Trevignano remains somewhat difficult to reach. From Rome just thirty miles away today's visitor takes the ancient Via Cassia—that same Via Cassia built by Roman soldiers—before turning onto what was until fairly recently a dirt track for horse carts. These six miles to Trevignano are still beautiful but intimidating to all but the most heedless driver. The narrow road is a green avenue of huge, picturesque trees, but notoriously dangerous. As the bunches of mourning flowers tied to trees from time to time testify, tragic accidents occur all too frequently. Sixty of these trees were recently cut down for safety's sake.

Cares drop away when the visitor walks into the old walled town, that *borgo* dating from the Middle Ages. On one side is the waterfront and a walkway paved with the cobblestones called *sampietrini* because they resemble those paving St. Peter's Square. On the other side still rises that stark cliff of rock, where houses are reached by climbing up narrow alleys and steep staircases. The town is beautifully conserved, thanks to the post-Orsini centuries of poverty.

Most of the authentic *Trevignanesi* families are related, and indeed many confusingly bear the same five or so villager names, beginning with Stefanelli and Marconi. These locals still drive tractors, still tend fields, still own shops, and still help run city hall. They still care, in short.

On weekends and especially in summer Trevignano is jam-packed with Roman city dwellers, out walking their dogs, basking in the clean air and sunshine, showing off their smart casual clothes, taking selfies and filling the cafés and restaurants to overflow. Increasingly, the town is also a permanent haven for a growing number of elite Romans, driven from their posh downtown apartments by potholes, pollution, Covid-19 and the corrupt politicians who sent taxes skyrocketing without providing services. A certain number of these commute to and from Rome each day, in defiance of the picturesque avenue of trees.

Strolling on the waterfront side by side, too, are countless vacationing visitors, from California to Australia. Many are retired here. Indeed, Trevignano sometimes seems overrun by savvy foreigners from all over the world, a place where in the lakefront cafés at midday mostly English tends to be spoken, with Irish, British, Dutch, German and Scandinavian accents. Of Trevignano's almost six thousand inhabitants, one thousand are foreigners, half of whom are fairly well integrated Romanians. Africans selling trinkets are regulars, and well known: "Hello, my black brother," a Trevignano workman greets one of these vendors; elsewhere these vendors are often reviled and sometimes physically attacked.

Not here: indeed, one, named Adam, was run down by a local Trevignanese who had been blinded by sunlight. In hospital two weeks, Adam was visited twice by men from Trevignano, who also took him a kitty of $220 for him and helped him find a lawyer.

Taken altogether, the town is both simple and straightforward, while at the same time remarkably sophisticated and cosmopolitan.

The heart of the attraction is the lake itself. Lake Bracciano is Rome's reservoir, which means that the water is tested frequently to check that it is clean enough to drink. Only a few gasoline-powered motor boats, such as the lone tour boat and the Carabinieri police boat which checks on fishing and boat licenses, are allowed. Water-skiing is not permitted, which brings safety; sports lovers can swim literally miles without risk of being struck by a speed boat. Here one can also fish, scuba dive, kayak, paddle board, sail and wind surf. Land lubbers play tennis, ride horseback, practice archery, learn to fly a plane, feed a hawk or eagle and, if truly daring, hang-glide from the highest point of the cliff overlooking the town.

The abundant traces of its long past are also readily visible. Some are obvious. An early Etruscan stone coffin made of tuff stands in the middle of the main piazza, hard by a gigantic marble chunk from the architrave of an ancient Roman temple. A very early medieval church, which incorporates vestiges of a Roman temple, leans against the late nineteenth-century town hall. Overlooking this from a hillside slope is a majestic sixteenth-century church, which happens to have been built atop the ruins of a Roman temple. Above that are the ruins of what began as an Etruscan fort and was then rebuilt into a powerful walled medieval fortress.

Just visible across the lake is one of the great Renaissance castles of Europe, built in 1470 by the powerful Roman family of the Orsini of Bracciano; here, in what is known today as the Orsini-Odescalchi Castle, Tom Cruise married Katie Holmes in 2006, in an event celebrated with a tiered cake supposedly as tall as Mr. Cruise himself.

Car parks before entrance to gutted Etruscan tomb—one of a thousand in Trevignano.

Local youngsters braved rain for hours in hopes of glimpsing the actor, but with no luck, for his limousine had one-way windows. (The couple divorced just six years later.)

Then there are the less obvious traces of the deep past, interwoven with the present. Overlooking a bus stop on the main road passing through the town center is a stretch of aqueduct built by the Emperor Trajan and centuries later partly destroyed by barbarian invaders. On our own street, Via della Macchia, the nose of a car snuggles into what looks like a cave but is in fact the entry into an ancient Etruscan tomb, long ago sacked and then turned into a pen for animals or for storage of crops. During wartime these empty tombs provided safe refuge from bombs.

In this, the heart of ancient Etruria, Trevignano and its neighboring hillside of Vicarello, three miles to the west, boast mineral-rich volcanic soil. The rich soil and the village's ideal position, facing south, have made it particularly well suited for farming. In addition, Vicarello is awash in hot springs whose medicinal properties were valued from earliest times; indeed, Neolithic arrowheads of obsidian, imported from Sicilian islands, have been found among ancient ruins there as offerings.

I came upon the lake and the town by chance. The editor of an American guidebook had assigned me to devise a series of driving tours outside of Rome proper. Since the book would appear the following spring, and the editors needed a long lead time for publishing, I had to do my research by touring in my car in November and deliver the text by Christmas. Day after day dawned cold and rainy, producing the sort of dull grey misery that makes you want to draw the covers over your head and stay in bed until spring. It was no easy matter to rhapsodize about a tourist venue when you can barely see beyond the swishing windshield wipers.

And then, twenty-five miles north of Rome, I came upon Trevignano. The fog lifted, and with it my spirits. In all the misery of driving I had seen no place as comely as this one-time fishing village entered through an ancient gate. Forgetting the assignment, I hunted out a real estate agency in the center of town. The agent had no objection to showing me, then and there, the plans for a small palazzo overlooking the lake. "Construction is almost finished, save for the top floor. We'll be doing that shortly," he said, shoving aside full ashtrays and empty coffee cups to unfold the plans.

"I'll think about it," I said cautiously.

A month later, the assignment complete, I returned. We climbed up steps and at last stood on a cement floor at the top of the building, where the penthouse was to be built. Across the lake was a view as pretty as any on the Amalfi coastline, or so it seemed to me.

"I'll take it."

"Sight unseen?" The apartment was still not built. The realtor seemed stunned.

"Sight unseen," I said, now reckless.

Amazingly, the top floor was finished in record time, and a few months later I took up weekend occupancy of my little penthouse atop the palazzo. Soon every one of the other eight flats was occupied, and—perhaps because no one knew anyone—we all became instant friends. On Saturday nights Roberta would shout up the staircase: "Who's for spaghetti? Luigi is cooking."

"Okay," I'd holler down the stairwell, "I'll bake brownies."

"I'll bring couscous," Mustafa, who was Egyptian, would yell from the second floor, where he lived with the pudgy and very Italian Antonio.

I was on my own for the first time in two decades after the painful breakup of a marriage, and so I was particularly grateful to attend a Saturday evening potluck. As the weather grew warm, our Saturday evenings spilled over into the soft jasmine-scented evenings of summer. Some Saturday evenings the little group would go for a walk after supper. One summer evening, we even went dancing in a lakefront outdoor bistrot. By then we all knew each other fairly well.

As I danced that evening with Mustafa, he mentioned that the parents of his pudgy partner Antonio were coming for a visit: would I join them Sunday afternoon for tea? "They're quite elderly," Mustafa added.

"Of course," I said. Secretly I was taken aback, for Romeo and Juliette paled by comparison with Antonio and Mustafa. From a working-class Catholic family in Milan, blue-eyed Antonio ran a shop selling what he called "natural products"—face creams of almond oil, soaps made from olive oil. Darkly good looking, slender, Mustafa was a practicing Muslim, who rigorously respected his faith, including the spiritual month of Ramadan, when Antonio too fasted to keep Mustafa company. How, I wondered, would two elderly Milanese Catholics deal with their son, not only in a gay partnership, but also in one that crossed the nasty border of historically antagonistic religions?

Over tea that Sunday it was clear immediately that Antonio's parents, visiting from the north of Italy, were elderly, but that they had obviously taken the relationship between their son and his Muslim partner in stride. I need not have worried, and, if anyone had cause for embarrassment, it was I for my needless concern, which was also perhaps curiosity. Theirs was the "True love" of the song which Bing Crosby crooned in a movie sailboat with Grace Kelly when I was a youngster, and whose lack had made me suffer. But in this case the true love was also that of Antonio's parents.

Our dancing evening took place more than twenty summers past, and since then Antonio's sweet white-haired mother and assembly line worker father have died. The men were still together, and still as much in love as they had been on the evenings when Mustafa made couscous for our potlucks. And it is a good thing, too, for Antonio, not yet sixty, had developed early Alzheimer's, and needed Mustafa to tend him. When we would all get together from time to time, Luigi still cooked spaghetti, and when Antonio failed to remember who we were, Mustafa beside him would gently remind him of our names.

Antonio smiled happily, even as the rest of us in our old Saturday evening potluck crowd wiped away a tear or two of affection for both, and deep gratitude for true love, whenever and wherever it can be found.

Not long after I wrote this, our beloved Antonio died.

Trevignano lives on. It has remained as beautiful as when I first saw it, a flower blossoming in the misery of a bleak November. Its little fountains are not grand, like those at Tivoli, nor can its Roman ruins compete with those at the ancient Roman seaport of Ostia. But it is a summation of lake, climate, town, history, hospitality, people and, not least, love.

Like a black swan, it is also a rarity. And also like black swans, the lake itself is an endangered species because the water level has shrunk drastically—in 2017, by six feet. The situation is improving, and one hopes that, despite climate change, these improvements will increase, so that this biography of the lake will remain a lyrical paean, and not an obituary.

2

Ghosts

Measure it one hundred times
and life is always the same old size

—Bracciano proverb

I am no stranger to the joys and hazards of lake water, albeit in a far different way, during my early life in Cleveland, Ohio. Growing up in the far western suburb of Bay Village, we lived close enough to the lake that on a stormy night I could hear the angry roar of the waves of Lake Erie as they punched against the cliffs of the shoreline. By daytime, when the lake froze, as it did regularly, visible in the far distance would be a feisty ice-breaker, forging a channel for one of the giant freighters that plied all five Great Lakes no matter what the weather.

Since even before the Civil War, Lake Erie had been the port of call for boats delivering the iron ore mined above Lake Superior. During the mid-nineteenth century winters that ore was occasionally delivered by sleigh. A century later Cleveland had twenty steel and rolling mills and blast furnaces, clustered around the broad valley of the winding Cuyahoga River. There the iron ore arriving from the north met and married the coal delivered by train from the pits of southern Ohio and Pennsylvania. This was steel manufacture at its most rewarding, for its mills supplied the wherewithal for the railroad tracks, not to mention the locomotives, that first helped to win the Civil War, then lay the tracks for the trek westward all the way to California.

Not surprisingly, the pollution level caused by the manufacture of tracks and trains and later of washing machines and dishwashers was devastating. In the years after the Second World War many parents forbade their children to swim in the lake. So acute was the pollution near the mouth of the Cuyahoga River where it flowed into Lake Erie that the river actually caught fire in the summer of 1952, when two bridges burned down and repairs cost $100,000. By the time a similar fire occurred on June 22, 1969, it caused so little commotion that the *Washington Post* wrote cynically the next day, "Flare-ups on the river are so common that this particular fire, which was extinguished in half an hour and did relatively little damage, barely made headlines in the local papers."

My years as an undergraduate at Northwestern University were little different: Chicago pollution was no laughing matter. Lake Michigan washed up against the

From Bay Village beach across frozen Lake Erie, Cleveland skyscrapers. (*Photo Wikipedia Commons*)

shoreline of the sprawling university campus, and, in the ten-minute slog between lecture halls, we would be half blown apart from the wind-driven snow rushing across the icy surface of the lake.

Life was better in summer, but the Great Lakes season is madly brief, brisk and breezy. It was a thrill to discover that, by contrast, the Mediterranean summer dawdles along. From mid-May it is a careless, sultry maiden sending rose petals adrift to perfume the air. This endures into early October, when mildew traces on the grapes in the misty low fields make them precious to the wine harvesters. Like that wine, the Roman summer is to be savoured. One must revel in it; let it seep into the soul.

I did not invent this love of the Italian summer, needless to say. The Tyrrhenian seacoast lies barely a half hour from where I write. Passing on the coastal road on his way to Rome, Charles Dickens was bowled over by "the gardens of the bright villages along the road … all blushing in the summer-time with clusters of the Belladonna." Belladonna: a lily that I now grow in a pot on my terrace overlooking Lake Bracciano.

At every time of day, in every season, our lake is picture-pretty—ours in my mind, at least, now that I have had a house overlooking that lake for over a quarter century. In the mornings the blue waters are usually calm, especially in summer, while becoming lively and choppy in the afternoons, when the wind normally rises, and clusters of sailboats from the seven scattered sailing schools make their appearance. A particularly rainy springtime two years ago brought a savage storm that damaged a road on the Trevignano waterfront and literally wrecked a small bridge. The water level in the lake rose unexpectedly higher than in many years, infuriating the managers who rent summer beach umbrellas and deck chairs, for they found themselves with almost no beach, if only briefly.

At another time, while walking out in a light but chilly drizzle one day with our big dog Bella, a sort-of English pointer, I was appalled at the sight of first a few and then dozens of dead fish on the shoreline. They seemed huge to me: many were two feet and others over three feet long. As I tried to keep Bella from excitedly jumping upon the stinking dead carcasses, one of the local fishermen remarked grimly, "Carp. Bottom feeders. Never seen anything like it."

One of the grimmer sights was of a carp at least a yard long, still gasping as it lay dying on the grey-black volcanic sand at the edge of the lake. Obviously he could not live long. Nearby a cluster of village men stood gaping.

"How sad," I exclaimed. "Whatever is killing all these fish?" By then I had seen at least thirty dead.

"Copulation," said one, nodding wisely.

"What! Do you mean reproduction?" I asked, incredulous.

"Sure. A biologist tested them and said it was stress after they'd mated. Wore them out, it did." He shook his head wearily, intimating that sexual relations were a heavy-weather duty which only the hardiest of the male species could fulfill.

"Really? My goodness!" I said. Then, starchy as a Victorian school marm, I resumed my walk until, pausing after a mile or so, I recognized a familiar foursome of men who fished in the same spot most mornings. "I just saw some giant carp, dying," I told them, breathless with concern. Curiosity trumping starchiness, I added: "The men on the beach looking at them told me that they died from stress from, er, reproduction."

A fisherman burst into sardonic laughter. "And you believe that?" he asked.

"Well, no."

"Personally I'm too old to remember that particular stress," another joked.

His cigar-chomping buddy was more somber. "We are convinced that pesticides and fertilizers are seeping into the lake from the big new hazelnut orchards on that hillside." He pointed toward the slopes rising toward the volcanic Monte Romano, looming behind us to the north. Hazelnut orchards are a relative novelty in the district, the result of the popularity of the chocolate flavored-hazelnut cream called Nutella, beloved especially (but not only) of children. Invented in Piedmont immediately after the Second World War, when chocolate was scarce, the creamy treat was thinned with cheap ground hazelnuts. Today, sold worldwide, with factories from Mexico and Brazil to Warsaw, Nutella consumes ton upon ton of hazelnuts, with the result that literally miles of hazelnut trees already surround Trevignano, and more are constantly being planted, with results which we shall see in chapter 16.

"Hmm. Well, I'll do an Internet search on carp death," I promised, thinking that I would fail.

In this way I learned that Lake Ontario once had the same problem of the mass death of carp. Canadian scientists offered two possible explanations. The first was that a certain bacterial form turns virulent when lake water rises to abnormal warmth, and attacks the carp. This was not our case, however, for both winter and springtime had been particularly long and cold. The alternative cause mentioned by the Canadian researchers was "environmental stress," which I read as pesticides and other forms of pollution, exactly as the cigar-chomper had said. Carp copulation had nothing to do with it. Nutella—that is, the intense doses of weed killer in the orchards—most likely did. *Death by chocolate*, I was thinking.

It might have been better if it were fish copulation, as we shall see.

Meantime I considered the possible reasons for the misunderstanding, which I assumed was verbal. After testing the dead fish, the lake biologist would have indicated the cause as "*stress ambientale*" (environmental stress). But in the minds of the first group of village men the words had misfired. The sole Italian word I could think of that could explain their misreading of "*ambientale*" is "*amplesso*," or coitus. Did the men gave the word a pseudo-scientific twist—they were talking to a biologist, correct? Perhaps what they heard was "*stress amplessale*."

It would not surprise me to learn that a Latin male had made such a mistake.

But never mind. The rival forces of life and death, of swans swimming purposefully, fish dying from our careless greed, and sex wherever the roving Roman male mind chances to light, were my own early morning takeout fare on the lake, and most certainly food for thought.

Behind my impulsive purchase of that first apartment was the fact that I had grown up in a village on the shore of another lake, in this case Lake Erie. In my childhood there our town was the same size as Trevignano is today, with just under 6,000 inhabitants. After I moved to downtown Rome to live and work in the Sixties, for literally decades I was a tenant in a centuries-old, princely palazzo dating from the Renaissance, just one

Beneath lone surviving castle watch tower, shadowy area traces line of medieval wall. Postcard *c.* 1900.

block off Piazza Venezia on Via del Corso, Rome's busiest and noisiest street. The grand museums and concerts of those Roman decades were enriching, but in its way life in Trevignano has provided an agreeable release from the eternally over-crowded Eternal City, with its three million inhabitants, ever more tourist-clogged sidewalks and ever more poisonous pollution.

The gradual move into the village on Lake Bracciano awakened an unexpected flood of memories. Both Bay Village and Trevignano are on lakes, and are at the same time similar and far different. Unlike volcanic Lake Bracciano, Lake Erie was gouged out by serial glaciers that left a series of ridges, which explain such local names as Ridge Road and North Ridgeville.

Both these Italian and American towns lie an hour or so by car or bus from a large albeit exceptionally different city, in my case the industrial city of Cleveland. Bay Village teetered between serving as a fairly upmarket dormitory suburb, and a town where ordinary people lived, worked and even farmed; when I was young we all tended our vegetable gardens, and one woman still kept a cow. Trevignano too has daily commuters into Rome, but nevertheless behind us on our Trevignano hillside lived a friendly Romanian–Italian family, who keep two donkeys (one visited us from time to time at night) and several goats. A few steps farther is a pasture, home to three handsome horses.

In Bay Village my family lived next door to the Lake Erie Nature and Science Center, which shelters, among other animals, foxes. On our street here too we see wild foxes from time to time, including in our garden.

Another memory in common was the day a blizzard swept in across the lake from Canada. The Bay Village school heating plant immediately broke down, and so we junior high school students were told to walk home as best and quickly as we could, through the slanted, blinding snow. No cars could pass on the road, fortunately, for we could not have seen them, nor they, us. In Trevignano snowfalls are rare, but one April a few years back a brutal blizzard left us literally snowbound, without electricity and only the fireplace for heat for three days, very Bay Village style. Overnight the violent winds had thrown up a wall of snow blocking our driveway from the outside, so that we could not open the gate. The snow had also built up a wall against the garage door, which similarly could not be opened. This was particularly ironic: the snow shovel was tidily kept inside the garage, which we could not enter.

What was to be done? Wait until May when it all melted? Back in Bay Village we youngsters exploited such events. In blizzard time my girl chums and I went door to door with our snow shovels, offering to clear the icy steps and front walk for a dollar. When the terrible blizzard hit Trevignano, two kindly Italians in their sixties miraculously came to dig us out, unasked, unpaid, so that finally we could make our way for the mile walk downhill and into town, to drop into a café on the piazza for a heartening, hot cappuccino.

The postman evokes another memory, albeit with variations. In the supposedly good old days before the First World War, Trevignano's white-bearded postman, Giuseppe Avincola (the Avincola are one of the town's historic families, present in Trevignano from the early 1700s), walked fifteen miles every morning to the closest neighboring town, Bracciano, to collect the mail.

This meant that, in the course of his career, his daily walk to and fro amounted to 207,000 miles, as calculated by a local newspaper. Eventually Avincola was given a donkey and cart, which was put to use in 1914 to drive the village recruits off to that "war to end all wars," to borrow the overly optimistic phrase of Woodrow Wilson. Postman Avincola was also remembered for reading the soldiers' letters to their illiterate mothers, left behind in Trevignano.[3]

No one needed to read the newspapers in any case. Until the nineteenth century in England the news was by tradition bruited about by the town crier, who customarily wore a grand-looking costume and plumed hat. Ringing a bell, he would go about shouting "*Oyez, Oyez, Oyez*", or "Hear ye," from the medieval French for "listen," followed by his crying, "God save the Queen."

There being no newspapers in Trevignano, his equivalent in the early twentieth century was Enotrio Fabbri, who literally shouted the news, every day, through the village streets. Fabbri had no plumed hat nor bell, but he had honor. He had been one of the hundred or so Trevignano youths carted off to fight in the First World War, and returned home in 1918 blinded in both eyes by a hand grenade. Despite this, Fabbri was one of the lucky ones; thirty-two other young men who were called up from tiny Trevignano died.

In this way, with his white stick, the blind Fabbri would tap his way into the rather grand century-old town hall, which stands in the main piazza just outside the big gate into the *borgo*. There someone would tell him the news, which he memorized.

One of Fabbri's six children might occasionally accompany him, but mostly he would make his careful way from the town hall into piazza and then, through that main city gate topped by a tall, square eighteenth-century clock tower, into the *borgo*. Fabbri had pre-blindness recollections of that main gate and the narrow streets in the relatively small oval-shaped town area, but helping him to find his way within the *borgo* were the breezes blowing through the smaller gates that gave onto the lake—so we are told by Pasquale Tridente, one of the most recent of the town historians.[4]

"His news report always began with his shouting the words, '*Si avverte er popolo*'" (Let the people be informed), Tridente tells us. "*Er popolo*": Romanesque dialect for "*Il popolo.*" For the Trevignanesi, his blindness made Enotrio trustworthy, and so he was also the citizen chosen to extract numbers during the lotteries held at New Year's and the last evening of Carnevale, before Lent would begin. He died at age eighty-six in 1974. By then, of course, a news stand sold newspapers and magazines.

In Bay Village one man still arrived riding in a horse cart to collect what he called, in a shout, "pepper eggs!" (paper, rags). But otherwise there were cars, like our own Model T Ford. Because we had this, my mother was drafted into being one of the town post deliverers in the Christmas season during and just after the Second World War, when the usual postmen were serving in the military. This was anything but easy, for my mother had somehow to drive, not in the proper driver's seat, but in the passenger seat to the right, steering with her left hand as she stopped at each letter box to deliver Christmas cards. Perhaps needless to say, there was fortunately not much traffic—no one had money for gas in those war rationing days.

Keeping us informed were the daily newspapers—the Cleveland *Plain Dealer* in the morning, the *Press* and the *News* in the evening. No shouting was involved in their delivery: the papers were merely rolled up and heaved across the lawn onto the doorsteps by the after-school paper boys. Over time I happened to work for all three newspapers. For the *Press* and the *News* I was a reporter, but my introduction into journalism had begun during a college summer vacation at the *Plain Dealer*, where I was put to work in the complaints department. Rarely were these about editorial policy, as I had expected, and hoped. Instead a typical complaint was that the paper boy's dog had pooped on the subscriber's lawn or front porch.

In today's Trevignano the news is published in a dozen national newspapers, but also bruited about in the village cafés throughout the day, for these are the centers of daily life. And this is what is lacking in Bay Village despite there being a huge village green and a shopping center with a café. In Trevignano, every morning at 7:30, when the newsstand by the parking lot in the piazza opens, people are already waiting patiently in a little line before they head into their favorite café. Here most people still read newspapers, and, by the politics of the paper purchased, you know whether or not you can be friends. Everyone has a cell phone, but these are usually used less to read the news update than to ask La Mamma what she is cooking today, or, alternatively, to explain why it is impossible to visit her that afternoon.

With or without their smartphones, the old ways survive, not least the laundry hanging outside the town's sole Gothic revival building. And many a hausfrau living on a top floor still drops down the rubbish or hauls the shopping up to her balcony by virtue of a rope.

Life is slightly more formal in the central piazza in Trevignano, Piazza Vittorio Emanuele III, named for that king whose long reign in Italy lasted from 1900 through 1946, or through the two ghastly world wars that ended in defeat for Italy and the end of royalty like Vittorio Emanuele himself. This piazza does not, as might be expected, lie inside the old walled *borgo*, but just outside its main gate. Surrounding a small green park in front of town hall is, on its lake side, a big parking lot shaded by gracious old plane trees that, depending upon where you park your car, you must try not to slam into. Extending beyond this is the paved waterfront area, where mothers rock strollers, and little children play ball or ride tricycles; from there a pier juts into the lake, where the lone boat that takes on passengers for a tour of the lake ties up.

On the serious side of the piazza are an elementary school and a bank adjacent to that nineteenth century town hall. A touching monument stands before its door, with photographs of the thirty-two village soldiers who lost their lives in the First World War, when Trevignano had a population of little more than one thousand. On the opposite side are photos of the sixteen who died in the Second World War. Sad to say, there was little new in this: during the Punic Wars after 218 BC, the Romans who then controlled Trevignano had drafted its local farm lads, fishermen and herders into battle against the forces of Hannibal, sending them to fight and to die in both Italy and in North Africa.

3

Eruption

By the time the old lady has a hump
She's left her past in memory's dump

—Bracciano proverb

To begin at the beginning, this is in essence the biography of a lake from the beginning—its geology and history, beauty and battlefields, sources and resources and, not least, its people.

Gazing across this broad, usually (but not always) placid tub of water, from my terrace I can see the three towns that encircle the lake. Directly below me is our own Trevignano Romano, the northernmost of the trio. Off to the right is the largest and most famous town, Bracciano (Roman soldiers knew it as Castrum Brasani), hunkered around its huge castle of grey stone. And to the left across the lake is Anguillara Sabazia, poised high on a bluff that juts into the lake. With their ancient watch towers, the three towns served for centuries as defensive outposts guarding the roads toward Rome.

The surface of what is Italy's eighth largest lake covers some twenty-two square miles, while its shoreline slopes downward gently, then suddenly plunges to a depth of 525 or so feet. Overlooking all is a single quiescent volcano high above Trevignano, Monte di Rocca Romano.

Another volcanic area is the Valle del Baccano, the vast valley on the Via Cassia, which connects to Trevignano. There, scientists tell us, its volcano was still erupting some 80,000 years ago. Lesser eruptions between that valley and Trevignano created the crater that became the tiny, delightful Lake Martignano, a favorite of Romans. Both the Baccano lake (drained in the nineteenth century) and Martignano perch on slightly higher land and, through underground aquifers, have flowed into Lake Bracciano for millennia.

Rival versions of the origins of our lake exist. For some scientists, an eruption at Vico, further north, left a depression in the surrounding lands that gave birth to Lake Bracciano. "Both are suppositions, of course," historian-cum-journalist Franco Scalise told me in an interview. Scalise is a descendant of an eighteenth century Trevignano family, and his mother was a town employee. For forty years, beginning as a youth in the fire brigade, Franco too worked for the same Trevignano town hall. "Growing up I

Across the serene lake from Bracciano, Monte Romano rises above Trevignano (*left*); opposite is Anguillara (*right*). (*Photo Judith Harris*)

became fascinated with the remnants of the historical documents in the town archives," he said—remnants because many were lost in a long ago fire and others, "by the stupidity of the bureaucrats."

Whereas Trevignano's lively waterfront of cafés and restaurants is disarmingly redolent of charm, the lake itself and its basalt surrounding cliffs speak of ancient violence. Lake Bracciano was born of what scientists call "tectonic collapse," when a gigantic magma chamber, emptied of its lava by millennia of exploding volcanoes, caved in upon itself perhaps 600,000 years ago. It was then filled, and still is, by rain-water flowing from the steep hillsides into the underground channels called aquifers. Its birth as a magma chamber left the lake more or less penny-round, save for a few inlets here and there, showing where volcanic eruptions had taken place. Surrounding the lake, especially at Trevignano, are stretches of the interior of the volcanoes that hove into view along the road approaching the town from Rome. One of these small, water-filled volcano craters formed an inlet, called the Gulf Le Pantane (The Swamps, also known as the Gulf of Cucumino), which lies a mile due east of Trevignano, and forces the road to make a half-circle detour around it.

The gigantic, steep and threatening cliffs behind Trevignano, the oldest of the trio of lake towns, were once the interior of these sideshow eruptions. "The igneous rocks that form the landscape of Trevignano are the most conspicuous evidence of all the volcanic activity that occurred, first in the vicinity of Vico and then in the Sabatine area," writes archaeologist Ida Caruso.[5] Vico, a nearby lake also of volcanic origin, lies to the north.

Just when all this happened is any scientist's guess. The discrepancies are amazing. Some say the lake was born out of violence years 300,000 years ago ago, others, one million years ago; others still give the date at just 150,000 years past. A few scientists believe that the lake was somehow once connected to the sea, for fish and shellfish typical of the salt water Tyrrhenian Sea have been found in the fresh water of the lake. However, others hypothesize that either the salt water fish were raised in the lake in ancient times by clever fishermen, or else some swam up the Arrone River, which connects the lake to the sea beginning at Anguillara. These tiny salt water shellfish feed a surprisingly large number of larger lake fish: trout, eel, carp and, introduced early in the last century, a delicate whitefish called *Coregone lavaretus* of the salmon family. Feeding upon these are countless aquatic birds, from hawks to herons, wild ducks, pigeons, black cormorants, crested grebes, coots, geese and huge seagulls with powerful wings (the swans are apparently vegetarians). In the water near the shore too are numerous animals, including river rats. Even beaver have been seen in a cove near Trevignano, presumed to have escaped from a den where they were being raised for their valuable fur.

Besides olive groves, among the many trees are oaks, cypresses, cottonwoods, umbrella pines, chestnuts—we have ten on our own land—and plane trees (sycamores), with their tantalizingly artful, multi-hued grey bark. All these trees shade the narrow road, beloved by Sunday cyclists, that encircles the lake. Portions of this road were used by the ancient Romans, but it was perhaps built even earlier, by the Etruscans, who had a city at today's Trevignano.

In places the original inner wall of a huge volcano is starkly visible. Hard by the gas station owned by the Palma family at the edge of town is a dramatically steep cliff of black basalt rock that soars hundreds of feet high. The inherent violence of that cliff is tempered by a tiny shrine, carved into the basalt, which I call the Madonna of the Rocks.

More basalt is visible along the Trevignano shoreline, where a half-mile-long retaining wall of gigantic black basalt boulders was built, obviously at considerable expense. These boulders were hacked out of the cliffs, by hand, in 1974, when the *passeggiata*—the walkway beloved of today's strollers—was being completed.

Its volcanic underground also explains the presence of hot springs at Vicarello, the estate which overlooks the lake three miles from Trevignano, and at Stigliano, some fifteen miles distant. The Vicarello baths are closed, but Stigliano's attract visitors, who lie leisurely in its naturally hot waters, as I have. To my eyes, these documents of the birth of the lake, the hot springs, the basalt rocks on the *passeggiata*, the sheer cliffs, are enchanting—even though in my imagination they never lose their aura of recording the ominous.

Opposite above: In Vatican Gallery fresco, Lake Bracciano with Trevignano *(top)* and Anguillara *(right);* Rome and Tiber Riber in the distance, *c.* 1580.

Opposite below: Thrust from the volcano innards, boulders of basalt used to build retaining wall at Trevignano shoreline.

Capranica
Sutri
Calcata
M.Rosi
Mazzano
Baccano
Viano
Campagnano
Scrofano
M Ritondo
Vicarello
Triuignano
Ischia
Martignano
Cesano
Formello
Oriolo
Lago di Bracciano
Isola ol Veij
C Ciubileo
Anio Fl
Anguillara
S.Giouanni
M Trano
Manciana Selua
Maesia Silua
ROMA
Sasso
Cornazzano
Ceri
Palidoro
S Seuera
Maccarese
Magliana

4

Twig brooms

On the trees of human pests
birds will always build their nests

—Bracciano proverb

The closer I look, the more I am amazed to see how much of the ancient world survives in our own world, and perhaps especially in today's Trevignano. In addition to the signals sent by the volcano itself, like those fearsome basalt cliffs, echoes of the deep past, and even of its daily life, immeasurably enrich daily life today: the stretch of an emperor's aqueduct overhanging two bus stops, the Roman wall in *opus reticulatum* which backs up against the town hall, the medieval castle ruins hovering on a hilltop above the town.

If these are, in the end, fairly obvious vestiges of the deep past, I came gradually to see beyond them. I even came to see that such a modest, homely object as the big twig brooms, which the workmen use every day of the week to sweep leaves into little piles for later collection in a truck, are in themselves survivors of the deep past. When I asked how it is possible that brooms made of twigs are still in use, the sweeper assured me solemnly, "These work better than any other broom I've tried."

I could only smile. Where else but along our lake would one find a broom, hand-made of twigs tied onto a stick with a bit of twine? (In fact, many other places: Mary Jane and Peter Bridges, Americans who lived many years in the heart of old Rome, recall sweepers at work with twig brooms in Rome itself until recently.) Still, this question raised another: who had invented this simple, useful tool, and when? It was easy to guess that it had to have been those people who first lived in a house with a floor. Even if made of trampled dirt or clay, that floor would have had leavings that eventually needed sweeping.

Then another and more intriguing question came to mind: just when did the people here first live in houses? The question had me off and running. As scholars know, and as I would soon learn, dwellings were made when mankind finally stopped hunting and gathering, and began a settled existence of raising crops and tending herds of animals. Their newly domesticated pigs, sheep and goats also needed shelter, so these too had to be built. This transformation, called the Neolithic Revolution, brought permanent

Sweeping leaves with twig broom, Trevignano Romano.

huts, clustered together—that is, the first villages. In addition, as an archaeologist pointed out to me, "The Neolithic was one of the great creative periods in human history. And creating a stable place to live was also the first time that man altered the natural environment." This was, in short, the beginning of civilization as we know it, and it occurred at different times in different places. In the Near East some scholars place this evolution from the hunting-gathering society as early as 9000 BC and, in certain areas of the eastern Mediterranean and Greece, to 7000 BC. From there the new developments moved fairly slowly toward western Europe. In Switzerland, for instance, around 4000 BC communities were formed with wooden houses on lake shores. These early stable communities changed the economy as well as the environment. What most call the Neolithic Revolution is called by historian Yuval Noah Harari the Agricultural Revolution, and so it was.[6] But it was also the Business Revolution, for once crops like wheat were grown, they could be sold, and were. So were the animals, down to and including the now extinct bovine aurochs, an ancestor of today's domestic cattle. To sell their wares, the Neolithic traders on Lake Bracciano built boats which could voyage down a narrow river from the lake toward a market at the Mediterranean shore.

The transformation from hunting-gathering to settled communities moved from the eastern Mediterranean toward Europe only gradually. Archaeo-botanist Ehud Weiss and his team from the Department of Land of Israel Studies and Archaeology (he holds a PhD in archaeology from Harvard) were excavating in 2004 at a site, Ohalo, formerly submerged in water by the shore of the Sea of Galilee in Israel. There they found the remains of 150,000 plants, including such foods familiar today as barley, wild wheat, almonds, pistachios, olives and figs. Those spectacular finds, dating from 23,000 years ago, offered an unprecedented menu of what was eaten by the people of the Upper Paleolithic (the late Stone Age, that is), which preceded the Neolithic. Starch remains found on a grindstone show that bread, made of wild einkorn and emmer, had been baked at the prehistoric site of Ohalo.

Most importantly, although this was a transition period for hunter-gatherers, Prof. Weiss and his team also discovered traces of huts that had been made of brush, as if for a temporary camp. In one hut they found the remains of the earliest bedding known to date, a grass mat placed upon a rudimentary floor near a hearth. In another hut was what amounted to a kitchen, where cereal grains were found near a grinding stone. "It's like we were able to open these people's cupboards," Prof. Weiss told *Archaeology* magazine."[7] Since then scholars have learned to open the cupboards of other Neolithic peoples, including on Lake Bracciano, only to discover that their lives in some ways resemble those of many in the nineteenth century, which was when the term "Stone Age" was coined. The Neolithic is now recognized as far less primitive than the existence which we had been accustomed to thinking. These were not cavemen: if even the hunter-gatherers had built huts for refuge, as we now know, the Neolithic man went farther, creating villages. Caves were often sanctuaries, like those I visited at Altamira in Spain, decorated with handsome paintings dating back as much as 35,000 years.

A precondition for the Neolithic farmer in his little village was having to learn how to make and to bake ceramic pots, for otherwise the foods he raised could not be preserved. This brought a nasty footnote, for skeletal remains have demonstrated that, because their diet based on cereals and dried fruits and legumes kept for months in pots, the people—still newcomers to village life—declined in stature because less nourished; the fresh foods obtained from foraging were healthier than those grown and kept, dried, for the winter, which helps explain the vogue for the paleolithic diet, which excludes cereals. In addition, the teeth of the Neolithic people showed decay. From living cheek by jowl with each other, they also caught previously unknown diseases.

Most unexpectedly I found that I was living next door to the most important Neolithic village ever discovered in western Europe. Only slightly younger than those in Switzerland, whose earliest villages date from 4000 BC, our lake village was larger. It was discovered underwater, at a spot which I see every day from my house in my own village. On the basis that no stone materials belonging to the Lower and Middle Paleolithic period have yet been found nearby, this makes the Lake Bracciano village the oldest sign of human life in the territory, according to archaeologist Ida Caruso.[8]

Federico Fabbrovich is an archaeologist who lives in neighboring Bracciano. During a lecture some time ago to a small group in Trevignano, he spoke of his adventures in excavating underwater in Lake Bracciano. The excavation he described had first begun in 1989, when workmen, dredging the lake bottom to lay pipes for a supplementary aqueduct to carry water into Rome, had ploughed through the mud layer lining the lake bottom right into what would later prove to be a Neolithic village hidden in an area known today as La Marmotta, near the Anguillara promontory on the southeast shore of the lake.

When the drill bit for the giant aqueduct tubes brought up fragments of obviously prehistoric pottery, aqueduct construction was immediately halted. The pottery, some painted and some decorated with seashell impressions, confirmed the findings as from the Neolithic period.

La Marmotta cove under Anguillara promontory, with aqueduct marker (*right*).

In Italy all treasures from excavations of this type belong automatically to the state, but initially the Roman cultural authorities were not overly exercised. Archaeologist Maria Antonietta Fugazzola Delpino, at the time director of the Luigi Pigorini National Museum of Prehistory and Ethnography in Rome's EUR district, was summoned to analyze the findings. Fugazzola, expert on Italian prehistory and a widely published author, had already supervised excavations in Lake Bracciano of several Bronze Age villages on stilts, submerged fairly deep underwater as a result of sudden and drastic rising of the lake level. One of these villages was at Vigna di Valle, near Anguillara, while the others were close to Trevignano, at neighborhoods today called Acquarella, Vigna Grande and Vicarello, of the hot springs.

Those villages were submerged because of a sudden rising of Lake Bracciano, perhaps caused by an earthquake. This upsurge of water has occurred at various times in Lake Bracciano; indeed, in addition to the Bronze Age villages on stilts, foundations of submerged ancient Roman villas are actually partly visible near the lake shore just west of Trevignano, where thieves have had a joy ride hunting ancient Roman artifacts.

The location of the La Marmotta village was important. In Italy, scholars say, the process they call "Neolithicization", or adoption of the burgeoning, imported agri-pastoral economy (i.e., raising crops as opposed to hunting-fishing survival), began in the Italian deep-south, at Puglia and Lucania, in the 6th millennium BC and from there moved slowly up the peninsula. However, the settlers at La Marmotta were obviously far more advanced than the locals. It was evident that they, and their fairly rich culture, had come from afar, reaching Lake Bracciano in boats rowed inland from the Tyrrhenian seacoast up the 3-mile-long Arrone River (5 km). That there were inhabitants well before the Marmotta people is known. The mild climate, the fresh water, the fish, the rich vegetation that fed animals which could be captured, the great number of hillside caves—all provided sustenance for very early people, as is shown by the findings of human bones and of flint arrowheads and knives, from periods yet to be seriously studied here.

How did the settlers at La Marmotta know to voyage up the Arrone? They did not necessarily arrive on the lake in a single voyage directly from the eastern Mediterranean; more likely, they had lingered at coastal settlements along the way before touching our shore. Vessels took travelers to and fro throughout the Mediterranean even in earlier times; in fair weather no port of call is farther than five hours of sailing time distant. At each port someone would have had to marry a local, learn the local language and deal with newcomers arriving by sea. At the river mouth here the wandering seafaring newcomers would have learned that the river led to a lake, of interest because its salt-free water would irrigate the crops they intended to plant, and knew how to raise and to harvest.

In 1992, three years after the first potsherds were spit up to the surface, government permits to begin proper excavations at La Marmotta arrived, and serious work began that April. But before anyone could see the actual site, a 9-foot layer of silt, which lay below 24 feet of water, had to be removed, using a powerful suction hose that resembled a vacuum cleaner. Working upside down, the diver-archaeologists descended. Fugazzola Delpino herself had to learn to dive.

An important question is just where this thick layer of silt had come from. One possibility is that, when a powerful earthquake rocked the lake (and earthquakes in this area are still frequent), it caused a phenomenon known as liquefaction, which occurs when tremors churn underground water and silt into a thick, dark sludge (technically, water-saturated sediment). This causes a sort of mud tsunami which, in the case of La Marmotta, permanently sealed in the quake-stricken village until our own time.

Archaeologist Fabbrovich, who began at La Marmotta in 1998, had already excavated at Pompeii and in Tuscany. More to the point, he had also excavated deep under water at Empuries, a submerged ancient Greco-Roman city on the Costa Brava in northern Spain.

"But this was absolutely different from anything I'd done before," he told me. "We couldn't always use flippers because they would have stirred up ever more mud."

Three months were required every year to remove the mud before proper excavating could begin. "Those first ninety days of removing the mud were tough. We had to be quick: at most we could stay underwater for only thirty or forty minutes. In April especially we'd come up with our hands and feet turned violet from the cold. We worked absolutely blind—we could see nothing at all so, besides the suction pump at the lowest level, we had to carry a light. We knew more or less how far we had to go under water, but then your bare hand would strike a rock or a piece of ceramic, or maybe even a post, and so your hand would get scraped and really hurt."

So that they would know where to begin work the next day, they laid a lattice of white pipes that eventually covered a swath measuring 165 by 135 feet. This was a relatively small section of the village, but nevertheless extremely interesting. As Fabbrovich admitted, "It was actually fun, strange to tell. Photographs don't tell the story. When you dive down, and see with your own eyes so much material—a carpet of ceramics, flints, pieces of wood, even scattered leaves from trees—it is thrilling, a totally unique experience."

Diving to excavate, underwater archaeologist at La Marmotta, Lake Bracciano. (*Photo courtesy Museo Pigorini*)

Tubby Neolithic Mother Goddess of soapstone, found at La Marmotta in Lake Bracciano, is under 2" tall.

origin of the settlers, are the ceramic cups and pots painted with typical parallel lines also found at La Marmotta.

Among the other spectacular findings were a number of attractively decorated opium pipes of clay, along with myriad semi-wild opium-poppy seeds, some carbonized. The archeology of the use of opium is of current academic interest, and some scholars believe that the seeds and pipes found at La Marmotta are the earliest evidence of opium poppy use in Europe. The poppy seeds found there are from a variety of the wild *Papaver setigerum,* which later became the domesticated *Papaver somniferum* known today. After those of Lake Bracciano, the next earliest findings of opium poppy seeds known to date were also in Italy, at Spilamberto near Modena, and dating from approximately the same period, between 5500 and 4800 BC.[10]

Whether in use for religious or medicinal purposes remains unknown.

What particularly fascinated me were, in addition, the findings of bones of at least two breeds of dog; of beads for a necklace; a milk whip; cups and pots of all sizes; and scythes with inserted sharp teeth for cutting grain. A series of extremely sharp knife blades were made of black obsidian, a volcanic glass that makes extraordinarily sharp knives and arrowheads, and could also be polished to make an early mirror; obsidian can be ground so sharp that it is still occasionally used in cardiac surgery.

The finding of a fair number of uncarved chunks of obsidian is also of particular interest. Each volcano produces its own type of obsidian, and hence its source can be identified. Those found at La Marmotta have been traced to the Aeolian Islands off Sicily and to the Pontine islands near Naples; in every case these could be reached only by boat. Scientists who analyzed samples via Particle-induced X-ray Emission (PIGE), and then from radiocarbon dating from contexts in southern Italy, place these in the 5th millennium BC.[11] The usefulness of obsidian made it valuable, and, because small and easy to transport, it just may have been used as a form of currency before the age of metals, when bronze began to be worked into lumpish coins. The obsidian fragments found at La Marmotta are thus considered an important contribution to the reconstruction of the prehistoric trade routes in southern Italy.

5

Stone Age stew

Place your order and do it yourself,
and you're served like a king

—Bracciano proverb

Alberto Pazzaglia, heir to the oldest bakery in Trevignano, once told me of making a bread he calls Etruscan, from white flour, hazelnuts and raisins. This gave me an idea: why not prepare an entire Etruscan dinner, and invite friends? The Etruscans settled on the lake at Trevignano around 800 BC, and we know that at least their wealthy enjoyed sumptuous banquets. But perhaps a Roman banquet would be simpler to concoct. Succeeding the Etruscans at Trevignano were the Romans—surely including the Trebonius family who gave the town its name—who dined reclining on cushioned benches. Albeit she was a female, the wealthy ancient Roman businesswoman Rutilia Polla, whom we shall meet later, held a monopoly on fish sales to Rome. At her estate overlooking the lake near Anguillara she famously entertained dignitaries: why couldn't I? In emulation, I had actually had a stone triclinium built on our lower terrace, for picnic fun. (Triclinium: three benches for reclining by the dining table.)

For details about the Roman banquets, I poked into the novel *Satyricon*, by Gaius Petronius Arbiter, who lived in the time of Nero. In it the fictitious Trimalchio, who is presented as a wealthy freed slave, enthuses over a meal of hare, "sows' udders," and fish in a spicy sauce. I would not eat hare and there was not much chance of shopping for sows' udders, but fortunately fish are readily available. And so are the green and black olives served in separate dishes. Sausages were also served, he recounts in chapter 31. The novel proceeds on to the libations: Trimalchio's diners washed down their meal with wine in carefully sealed bottles, whose labels bore the words, "OPIMIAN FALERNIAN 100 YEARS OLD." At this Trimalchio sighs, saying, "Wine has a longer life than us poor folk so let us quench our thirst." It was surely boastful that Trimalchio's century-old wine came from the territory of ancient Falernia, which came from Lazio south of Rome near the Campania border. My guests would have to make do with the more realistic wine from the Faliscan territory, part of ancient Etruria, which lay just down the road near Viterbo. I selected the most famous of these wines, Est! Est! Est!, so called because the German bishop Johnnes Defuk, a wine lover traveling to the

Neolithic pirogue surfaces in Lake Bracciano at La Marmotta. (*Photo courtesy Museo Pigorini*)

Vatican to meet the Pope in the year (easy to remember) 1111, told his scout to write "Est" (it's here) on the door of a tavern which offered excellent wine. At Montefiascone, 36 miles north of Trevignano, the over-excited (and perhaps tipsy) scout wrote it on the tavern door three times with exclamation points: Est! Est! Est! Or so goes the story.

Among the Romans interested in food there were also pragmatists. In a famous passage, the historian Varro, who lived in the 1st century BC and wrote about agriculture, explained, "*in Etruriae locis aliquot*"—that in various places in Etruria (which of course included Trevignano), the local soil was so rich that the cereal harvest was half again larger than elsewhere. Varro also mentioned wild asparagus, like those in bunches I buy every springtime from a cross-eyed young man, who spirits them out from the woodlands on the Rocca Romana above us. "They've become hard to find," he told me last spring. "The wild boar like them, and to hunt them you have to bend down and follow the trails through the brush that the boars have made. And hope they've missed a few." And missed you, I was tempted to add, as you plunged through the rough underbrush.

But then I had second thoughts. My growing curiosity about ancient foods plunged me farther back in time, and into byways that were occasionally bizarre. As I soon learned, a passion for ancient foods is anything but original. A quick Internet search churned up any number of diets advertised as healthily "Neolithic," and even the names of cookbooks purporting to offer Stone Age recipes. Some of these recipes supposedly derive from the earlier Paleolithic, or Old Stone Age. So popular nowadays is this

Paleolithic diet, which excludes carbohydrates and milk, that it was thoroughly scorched in mid-2018 by Jane Brody of the *New York Times*, who derided it, saying that the Mediterranean diet is superior.[12]

Behind this sudden (and to me surprising) interest in the deep history of foods is the fact that, since the 1970s, nutritionists have argued that we would be better off by adopting "the caveman diet." In her article "Prehistoric Dining: The Real Paleo Diet," which ran in *National Geographic*, Rebecca Rupp dubbed the Neolithic era the "civilized tail end of the Stone Age."[13] Forget chicken nuggets and potato chips, advises Rupp, who has a PhD in cell biology and biochemistry, and just "sync with the evolutionary roots by eating only what our ancient ancestors ate: meat and fish, fruits and vegetables, eggs and nuts."

Actual evidence of "Paleo" foods have been found in Spain, where an image on the wall of the Cave of the Spider (*Cueve de la Arana*) in Valencia depicts an individual climbing a tree to collect honeycombs, which he stuffs into a basket. Another example of Old Stone Age food comes from a cave called Grotta Paglicci, in the Puglia region in southern Italy, where a sandstone tool was found in 1989. Archaeologists believe this tool was used to grind the seeds of wild oats (*avena*) into flour; its probable date: 30,000 BC. Was this for unleavened bread baked on a stone slab over the fire in a hearth? It is more than likely.

The Neolithic Revolution in food also pumped up our brains, according to an article in the *Proceedings of the National Academy of Sciences* by Suzana Herculano-Houzel, a Brazilian neuroscientist at Vanderbilt University. For her, the success of the human brain—what made it superior to that of an ape—came about because earliest man (woman?) learned how to cook, rather than to eat only whatever could be stripped from plants and trees. Because digesting raw foods consumes an extraordinary amount of energy, the energy savings from humans dining on cooked foods permitted the expansion of the human brain.[14] This called for a prior step, however. Exactly as Neolithic food preservation depended upon the invention of clay pots (which actually already existed in Paleolithic times), before food could be cooked, humans first had to know how to make a fire:

> With its high metabolic cost imposed by its large number of neurons, [the human brain's evolution] may thus only have been possible because of the use of fire to cook foods, enabling individuals to ingest in very little time the entire caloric requirement for the day, and thereby freeing time to use the added neurons to their competitive advantage.[15]

To travel accurately that far back in culinary time is obviously difficult, however. Written records of ancient foods exist, but material evidence is generally hard to come by, for the simple reason that foods are perishable. Their study by archaeologists is therefore, while surprisingly popular, still a fairly novel subject; and their analysis is of necessity limited. Food provision was "a primary occupation of most people in ancient times," but prehistoric foods survive only in "extreme circumstances," writes Prof. Delwen Samuel of King's College London, whose specialty is the archaeology of plants.[16] One such extreme circumstance was the finding of Otzi the Iceman, the 45-year-old hunter who was killed some 5,300 years ago, and whose frozen, mummified body, now in a museum in Bolzano, was found in an Alpine glacier in the South Tyrol back in 1991. It literally made headlines worldwide when Viennese scientists discovered, from his intestinal contents, that the last meal of Otzi the Iceman was probably a snack of einkorn wheat and dried fatty, bacon-like goat meat.

The findings at La Marmotta date from the Stone Age but do not reflect today's Paleolithic diet, as is shown by the fact that the food residue found in pots rescued there showed multiple seeds and grains. The numerous objects sealed beneath those 24 feet of water and 9 feet of silt in Lake Bracciano—the milk whip, clay pots, plates and cups, grinders, the bones of pigs and goats, the sickles with wooden handles used for cutting grain—contain amazing revelations about the real Neolithic diet, two millennia before Otzi. The bones of pigs and goats, for instance, showed they had been slain quite young, and hence for food, according to Mario Mineo, archaeologist and curator of the La Marmotta collection in the Pigorini Museum.

Detailed chemical analysis of the residue at the bottom of terra cotta vessels showed traces of fruit and the seeds of wheat and barley, and of bones as well as cereal remains. Residue at the bottom of one La Marmotta pot showed that it had contained a stew of spelt and either venison or wild boar. This evidence of Neolithic stews proved to be as old or even older than any similar food evidence ever found. The vision of daily life these objects evoke has enough elements in common with our own life that I realized that, instead of a Roman or Etruscan banquet, I could prepare, in my kitchen, a Neolithic banquet to offer our friends. We already had our own olive oil and local wine. La Marmotta would suggest the rest.

Upon learning of our prehistoric village I had been thrilled, not least because from my terrace I could look out and see the village in my mind's eye—see it, imagine the people living there, imagine their looking at the same lake in its different hours, its waters sometimes shimmering, sometimes sulking. My imagination had carried me from twig broom straight into a two-story Neolithic house in a village that was a precursor to Trevignano. In my mind's eye I could see the houses, the fishermen in the lake, the farmers tilling the fields and harvesting what they grew. I could see the women weaving, tending babies and, not least, cooking over a tiny fire lighted in the hearth in the middle of the hut and then, after the meal, sweeping the dirt floor with a twig broom. From there, because so many of the foods I prepare differ only slightly from those of the Stone Age, I soared right back again through the millennia and found myself once more in my own kitchen—and gazing once more out at the lake which had hidden La Marmotta for almost 8,000 years.

Today's Trevignano has remained something of a farm town. Tractors slow down the traffic, and vegetables and fruits straight from the fields are sold directly from the back of the farmer's truck or from a stall mounted outdoors on the weekly market day. Obviously these foods are healthier than those shipped from afar, stored for weeks and perhaps sprayed with a preservative. Cheeses here are made from the milk of sheep and goats grazing on the hillsides. Pork is from local pigs and sausages, from wild boar. "Do you want fresh eggs from my hens?" whispers the lady at the checkout counter of the supermarket. From under the counter she pulls out a half dozen.

The restaurant food in Trevignano is anything but fancy. Forget *nouvelle cuisine* and tiny portions served on an outsized square black platter decorated with flower petals and balsamic vinegar swirls. In case you missed the point, the jokey simplistic name of one popular lakefront restaurant in Trevignano was "FUUD." The name of the game is simplicity: home-grown vegetables, grilled lake perch or *coregone*; tiny lamb chops roasted on a spit; spaghetti *all'Amatriciana,* with a sauce of tomato and bacon bits sprinkled with spicy grated cheese from the milk of ewes. Plainly, many of the foodstuffs we enjoy here now, beginning with the fish caught that very morning in the lake, differ little from those of the past: consider the finding, in Sweden, of 9,000-year-old fish preserved by the cold in a lake near the outlet of the Baltic Sea. Archeologists at Lund University reported that after harvesting, the fish had been cured with seal fat and pine bark, then wrapped in the skins of seals and wild boar, and finally buried in a pit covered with mud—exactly as the La Marmotta village was sealed in mud, and Pompeii, sealed in dust and pebbles that, with water, became a light cement.

This makes the little-known underwater village visible from my window all the more intriguing, for it provides us one of history's earliest actual recipes. It also opened what was, for me, a great big can of academic worms. Excited at the idea of Neolithic foods, I visited the Pigorini National Museum in Rome's EUR district, where the 100,000 artifacts of La Marmotta, including that fascinating opium pipe, are kept. A number of objects are on view but the vast majority remain in storage and are yet to be studied.

There I spoke with Mario Mineo, curator of the La Marmotta collection. Like Federico Fabbrovich, he had personally excavated the underwater village and is a particular expert on its pirogues. After Mineo showed me the pot containing spelt and deer or boar residue, I decided I would tell my guests what I had learned about this Stone Age site, indicate its position in the lake to the guests, and then put an appropriate dinner on the table on the terrace overlooking the lake. I already had an earthenware pot that could go into the oven. As for the stew itself, venison was not available (and I would not eat it anyway), but local shops sold the meat from wild boar. I knew a certain amount about boar, which have recently been seen even in Trastevere in downtown Rome. Returning home one evening after dark, on our own road I was stunned to see a gigantic, ferocious-looking mamma boar cross ahead of a file of eight cute babies (the mother can produce up to ten). I was less amused when wild boar broke into our garden one night so as to romp, damaging rose bushes as well as the wire fence. Worse still, the car of a woman driving too fast up our narrow road actually hit a boar. Whether or not the boar was seriously injured, her car was. When I mentioned this to a friend in Trevignano, he laughed. "Why, I've seen them foraging right in the main street here," he said. "They like to eat the garbage." Similarly, while visiting Hollywood, we had seen wild coyotes in a main road. My sister, Nancy Newberry, had often hosted an injured young bear on a porch at her North Carolina mountain home, and was criticized for doing so; someone later killed the bear. Like the Los Angeles coyotes and the North Carolina bears, the boar invasion of our countryside is deemed dangerous, and farmers claim that the local boar damage cost them almost $4 million in just one year, 2016.

"These animals are simply out of control," says the president of the agricultural association Coldiretti Roma e Lazio. "Out hunting for food, they devastate our harvests and wreck farm buildings."

Not surprisingly, therefore, wild boar are a favorite of licensed local hunters, who are allowed at certain times in the winter season to shoot them. No less surprisingly, boar sausages are popular here, as are the egg noodles called *pappardelle*, traditionally served with a spicy wild boar sauce. The symbol of the Ente Maremma, a public agency devoted to development in the area of Tuscany and Lazio, is a wild boar with a spear in its back, suggesting that the only good boar is a dead boar. Some Lazio regional towns, moreover, hold weekend festivals celebrating wild boar meat. These festivals are called "*sagre*," despite the fact that the word, which derives from the Latin *sacrum* or sacred, has religious overtones.

To respect the Neolithic recipe from La Marmotta, the grain called spelt was required to go with the boar sausages. Like boar meat, spelt—*farro* in Italian—can be purchased in our local shops, where it is today something of a pricy, up-market novelty. Spelt is a naturally generated hybrid of *triticum genus* (that is, wheat), which nature crossed long ago with two other ancient grains, emmer and something called goat grass. For over eight thousand years, the DNA of spelt, or *triticum spelta,* remained unchanged. The Etruscans and Romans ate it in porridge; well before them, the ancient Egyptians dined on spelt, as is shown by residue found in pots in delta settlements on the Nile. That residue was dated by archeologists to around 4000 BC, which, I noticed with pride, was at least a millennium later than our own La Marmotta spelt in the pots in the museum at EUR.[17]

For further elucidation about spelt I again turned to Varro, the ancient Roman agriculture expert. "The part of the spelt harvest which you wish to have ready for food should be taken out in winter to be roasted at the mill," he wrote, adding with business-like cunning: "If it seems likely to spoil, don't hold on to it—go ahead and sell it."

That was perhaps easier in Varro's time. In recent decades, its high costs made selling spelt difficult. Spelt grains are protected by a thick husk, whose removal is time-consuming and hence expensive, hiking up the costs of storage as well as transport. Moreover, once the hulls are removed, a bushel of finished spelt weighs only 30 pounds whereas ordinary hybrid wheat, with a hull half the size of that of spelt, produces 60 pounds of finished wheat—twice the amount of spelt.

This began to change when newly food-hip westerners, turned off by bleached white flour, began to seek out healthier foods. Despite its relative expense, spelt suddenly became prominently displayed on the shelves of specialist food stores. Easier to digest than ordinary wheat, rich with fiber, spelt attracted those who suffer from wheat intolerance and non-celiac gluten sensitivity. Today spelt is popular to the point that a recent newspaper ad promoted a "frozen spelt mini-burger, for cooks wanting speed as well as the healthiest of foods."

For my Neolithic banquet, I purchased spelt at the supermarket and, from a butcher shop, the wild boar sausages, which I planned to cook separately and then add in thick slices. For seasoning I could pluck laurel leaves from the bush by the driveway.

As for side dishes, I tried to envision the other foods available to the settlers at La Marmotta. From archaeologist Fabbrovich I had learned that those found there included lentils, peas, chickpeas and turtle remains (remember turtle soup?). In fact, roast turtle was in the Paleolithic diet, but that was literally reaching too far for my taste buds. Still, as I learned, the La Marmottans dined on cherries, strawberries, apples, hazelnuts, pears and figs, like those growing in abundance on my own sprawling fig tree.

In ancient Mesopotamia onions and white carrots were also staples, and garlic too was used, so I arbitrarily decided that most likely the Neolithic diet included both. As side dishes to the stew would be chestnuts, collected from our chestnut trees and roasted in the microwave oven (!) I also learned that green Swiss chard (*biete* in Italian, and which has nothing to do with the Swiss) was cultivated by the ancient Greeks, especially near the Mediterranean sea, and would do service as another side dish. Given its nutritious contents, chard is, like spelt, currently enjoying a major foodie revival, served alone or, as I planned to make it, quickly sautéed before dousing it with *parmigiana*; for cheese is another Neolithic food, as the tools for making it found at La Marmotta have shown. Indeed, at the town of San Giovanni in Persiceto, near Bologna, archaeologists found a sort of cheese factory dating from *c.* 6000 BC, only slightly earlier than the La Marmotta settlement. Scholars agree that cheese-making dates from the Paleolithic era, prior to the Neolithic, and point out that the Latin word *coagulum*, meaning rennet, is still in use in Lombardy and Emilia for curdling cheese.

Spelt stew laced with wild boar meat, vegetables, a cheese tray, figs: this, then, was the menu for my Neolithic dinner, to be served on ceramic plates appropriately made of glazed baked clay. After sunset, the table would be lighted solely with candles or by the light of the moon—that same moon seen by the La Marmotta villagers. At last all this was settled, and I could concentrate upon the table setting, the guest list, with invitations sent as emails and via WhatsApp. Just one thing remained to resolve. Whatever were my guests and I to wear? Perhaps authenticity could be taken a step too far.

6

Etruscans

He with few coins is always counting,
He with a gorgeous wife is always singing

—Bracciano proverb

It was a weeknight in the summer of 1993, and I had only recently moved into my small top-floor apartment at Rigostano, a half mile from the village center at Trevignano. The other occupants were away, and so I was alone in the building. As I dozed I became vaguely conscious of a humming noise that seemed to come from the nearby main road toward town.

Wrong. That morning, clambering down the staircase to head for a café, I saw, hard by the entrance to the side of the building, a gaping hole in the ground. It was a tomb—an ancient tomb. Without realizing what was going on, I had heard tomb robbers digging with some kind of a machine tool. The police came, but of course they were too late. Whatever grave goods the looters had found were gone; and perhaps already being sold to collectors. I subsequently learned that back in 1987 a number of important Etruscan chamber tombs dating from the late eighth and early seventh centuries BC had been discovered in the surroundings. In addition, archaeologists had also uncovered a system of ancient Etruscan wells and tunnels that had been dug through the volcanic tuff rock in order to divert a stream away from the farmers' fields. That looted tomb was one of perhaps one thousand Etruscan tombs that lay underground on the fairly steep slopes of the hills that rise for a mile or so on either side of today's town. Their sheer numbers show the importance of Trevignano in the age of the Etruscans. Even before the Etruscans settled there Trevignano had existed and even prospered. Their predecessors were the people living in central Italy known as the Villanovans, sometimes also referred to as Umbrians. They took their name from the tiny town of Villanova near Bologna in north-central Italy, where they were first identified in the mid-nineteenth century. This was the late Bronze Age, and their culture spread throughout the Italian peninsula from Emilia-Romagna in central Italy all the way down to the isle of Sicily.

Villanovan villages cluster around Lake Bracciano. One of these lay just off Vicarello, 300 yards from the present shoreline, and submerged by as much as thirty-three feet of water. Aerial photographs show that during that period the shoreline curved outwards,

Wild boar painted on Etruscan–Corinthian vase, seventh century BC, in Trevignano Civic Museum.

but at some later point the lake's volcanic nature took over, as it had at La Marmotta centuries earlier, causing the lake waters to rise and engulf that village.[18]

Villanovan settlers had occupied the hillside at Trevignano itself. Their traces may some day be found submerged in the lake, but in the meantime archeologists discovered tombs identified as typically Villanovan, in the shape of both wells and ditches, just off the Via della Macchia, the narrow, winding road leading to our home, which overlooks today's (and yesteryear's) town. Found in those tombs in 1910 were a bronze *fibula*, or brooch, which vaguely resembles a safety pin; a bronze lid for a terra cotta pot that had presumably held ashes; and a woman's necklace composed of amber and glass beads. Etruscan tombs were also found there in 1991. What especially gave me pause was the difficulty in driving the half-mile up the tortuously narrow Via della Macchia. The geology of the harsh volcanic rock makes its hairpin curves and uphill route obligatory, and dangerous. Little has changed this road over time. A footpath inaccessible to horse carts until the 1820s, it was roughly covered with tarmac less than a half century ago. Even today those tight curves, overshadowed by rock, remain a challenge for cars, as well as a steep climb for hikers.

The Villanovans were among those plodding uphill on that very same twisting path which I often walked. The area being part of their necropolis, up that same footpath they would have carried the ashes or the bodies of their loved ones, who included the woman who had worn the necklace of beads of amber and glass found in her tomb. I wondered how she had died—was it in childbirth, or was she herself little more than a child? Her necklace did not give me an answer. But as I walked up that same steep hill to my home, where Etruscan tombs lay on either side of our olive orchard, for just a moment I shared in the mourning for her loss.

Following the Villanovans were the Etruscans, whose arrival from the eastern Mediterranean to settle initially in what is called "Old Etruria" ended the Bronze Age. The chief reason behind this transformation was again technological: the passage from fusing bronze to working iron. The new material was less expensive and easier to mine than copper ore and its alloys. Most importantly, ploughs and daggers of iron were stronger than those made of bronze, which is to say better for both farming and military defense (and offense). The result of the Iron Age was what came to be called the Etruscan civilization. Driven by the search for iron ore, it was the product of a melting-pot in which local inhabitants and their ways were merged with innovators from any number of far-away places in the eastern Mediterranean, particularly Greece but also Egypt and Lebanon.

It happens that by the seaside, a half-hour drive from Trevignano by today's reckoning, was the little town of *Caisra* (*Caere* to the Romans, today's Cerveteri). Graced from time immemorial with three small, convenient harbors, it had, just inland, hills rich with iron ore. After about 1000 BC the iron ore rush drew sailing vessels from the eastern Mediterranean all the way around the Italian peninsula and then half-way up the Tyrrhenian coast to Caisra. From there the early Etruscan culture spread inland, to Trevignano and its neighboring towns north of Rome like Veii. This was close to the beginning; after 750 BC the Etruscans would advance beyond the Tyrrhenian area north of Rome, and upon Rome itself, before spreading onward to the Po Valley in the north and to the Campania in the south. As a result, as Etruscologist Caterina Pisu points out, between the eighth and seventh centuries BC life in Italy was radically transformed with a surge in population and a "framework of political, social, cultural, technological and economic change," particularly evident in Southern Etruria.[19]

The new wealth reflected and increased trade, which necessitated the expansion of road networks. By the eighth century BC near Trevignano were fourteen neighboring towns. The growth of trade and roads increased the importance of transportation, which explains why two- and four-wheeled horse-drawn carts (parts of two are visible in the Trevignano civic museum) were given places of honor in the tombs of the powerful, including at Trevignano.

Trevignano was a reflection of the Etruscan Iron Age, but it was bicultural. Seventeen miles to the west was the powerful Etruscan town of Veio, near Caisra (Cere), close to the sea and to the iron-ore hills. The Veio territory, which dominated Trevignano, was ever more strongly influenced by the new arrivals from the eastern Mediterranean, and its artifacts are described as "orientalizing." By contrast, eight miles inland to the north of Trevignano was Sutri, whose people (the Etruscans called them *feluskes*) and culture were Italic.

The thousands of artifacts found in the Iron Age tombs in Trevignano reflect both cultures. A magnificent black-figured amphora found in the Annesi Piacentini Tomb in the Olivetello neighborhood was typically Corinthian, whereas a trapezoidal standard typical of the Faliscans was found in the princely tomb called the *Tomba dei Flabelli* (Tomb of the Fans). In the words of archaeologist Pisu, who has made a thorough study of the archaeology of Trevignano, the town was a "bridge" between the two cultures, that of Greek-influenced Veio and that of the Italic Faliscans at Sutri. For Ofelio Maciucchi, the author of seven books on the town history, Trevignano served as a "sort of corridor" between Sutri and Lake Bracciano.

The Faliscans had their own proto-Latin language. In the Etruscan territory, their fundamentally Greek culture showed in their written language. The Etruscans wrote in a zigzag from left to right and then right to left. Their known vocabulary is limited because most of their surviving writings were found on grave markers carrying words like, "Here lies the beloved wife/husband." Even so, over three hundred Etruscan words are known, written in a 26-letter alphabet that closely resembles Greek lettering; and when I took a course in Rome on "Etruscan language and literature," my fellow classmates, all Italians who had studied Greek at school, were miles ahead of me, enjoying only the merest smattering solely of Latin. That alphabet reached the early Etruscan heartland in about the eighth century BC and was a "phonetic adaption" of the real thing. It was terrifically important for the Etruscan aristocrats, who used it as a tool of power and for trade.

Among the towns of Old Etruria (from that name, the area is still known as La Tuscia), Trevignano was particularly attractive to the newcomers just as it had been for the Neolithic and Bronze Age farmers, and for the same reasons. Unlike Caisra and its neighbor, Tarchna (Tarquinia), Trevignano offered abundant fresh water for irrigating crops, mineral-rich volcanic soil, lake fish for the taking, and plentiful game in the woodlands. The climate has always been particularly favorable; facing south, the hillside is bathed in sunshine. Because the lake is ringed by a ridge of hills, moreover, crops were (and are) protected from the more savage winds that sweep in from the north. Although definitive proof of the precise location of Etruscan Trevignano is lacking, there is no doubt that the town was particularly important in its Etruscan centuries, and

Etruscan sarcophagus, 7th century BCE, Trevignano main piazza.

most experts today believe that it was the ancient Sabate, the town that gave the lake its original name. Sabate may have been situated on one of the higher slopes by the hill above the present town, where fortresses have stood since at least Etruscan times. If the settlement was lower, it may have been destroyed by the builders of the later Roman aqueduct, for the space between the steep slopes and the lake was, and is, narrow. Alternatively its ruins may lie underwater. At any rate, in the middle of the grassy space in the town's main piazza today are two artifacts that testify to Trevignano's Etruscan past: sarcophagi of rough tuff stone, dating probably from the seventh century BC. Two of the cave-like tombs so far discovered were the burial places of princely families. At the Annesi Piacentini Tomb in the Olivetello necropolis, where its chambers were dug into tuff, four funeral beds were found; upon each were piled ten bodies, one skeleton atop the other.

At our own Via della Macchia, at the bottom of the road is an empty tomb, whose entryway is used as a cozy place to park a car. And just a block away is a stretch of Etruscan aqueduct, later incorporated by Trajan into his, necessary to slake the thirst of his Roman subjects. When we moved in 1995 on to that street a half-mile uphill, just outside our driveway entrance was a cave-like Etruscan tomb. On a neighbor's property, it looked like a big hole in the ground. Alas it was an empty hole, long since stripped of its grave goods. The new owners of the property happened to be contemporary Romans unaware of the Etruscan tombs all around us, and by the time I mentioned to them that one lay on their property, they had already filled it in with rocks and dirt to make more space for their flower garden and barbecue.

Born in Trevignano Romano, Ofelio Maciucchi (1925–2006) was the author of seven books on the town history. (*Photo courtesy Massimo Maciucchi*)

The Etruscan town at Trevignano endured for at least (and probably more than) four centuries, scholars believe. According to the late town historian Ofelio Maciucchi, by the seventh century BC the Etruscans of Trevignano hustled their wine, olive oil and grain throughout the Mediterranean. With them from the eastern Mediterranean they had introduced "Hellenization" into the local culture. Tomb offerings which illustrate this Hellenistic (orientalizing) influence have been found during the past forty years or so, in at least four areas of Trevignano, including at Rigostano, where today's Recostano Residence hotel-gym complex is located.[20] The tombs themselves were entered via a descending narrow corridor called a *dromos* that leads into a chamber carved out of the soft volcanic tuff rock. Most of these tombs were located between Trevignano and Vicarello; few are found elsewhere around the lake.

Maciucchi's contribution to the town's history is especially important. Born in Trevignano, he worked in Rome but remained constantly in contact with his native village. After studying its deep history for a decade, he produced seven books on town history. In the words of his son, lawyer Massimo Maciucchi, "He had a deep, visceral and poetic love for his native town."

Besides iron ore, other minerals drew the newcomers from the east, writes Maciucchi. "The mineral-rich mines in the mountains at Tolfa, Monte Amiata, the island of Elba and the Rognosi chain provided what was in great demand in that era: zinc, silver, copper, tin and lead." Thanks to this, links between the Etruscans and the various other peoples of the Mediterranean were formed.

"From the eighth century onward the trade between Etruria extended from central Europe to the eastern Mediterranean, which sent, in exchange for the crude metal ores, made objects of high quality, until the penetration of the new experiences were assimilated into the regions with a high cultural level, and permitted the beginning and development of a local artistic activity," Maciucchi concludes.[21]

Countless of the Etruscan tombs, including those near me, have long since been looted. Especially in the nineteenth century, when farmer's ploughs routinely broke into the tombs, the farmer would pocket whatever was made of gold and toss away the rest, beginning with the vases of terra cotta. When new houses were being built frequently in the 1980s and 1990s, the grave offerings were sold to collectors, but, fortunately, a goodly portion has survived despite the looting. Almost four hundred artifacts found in those tombs are on view in the town's Civic Etruscan Museum, where they speak to us of the lives of the Lake Bracciano Etruscans. Illustrating a certain degree of the importance of the town in the Etruscan world, these exhibits include pieces of gold jewelry; objects made of bronze and iron; painted vases and pots that show a Corinthian influence; and other vases of various types and materials. A number of museum artifacts also demonstrate the settlement's connection with Veii, the early and very important Etruscan city of which Trevignano was a suburb. The pieces of two carts in the museum are pragmatic signs of the thriving Etruscan town. One was a chariot (*currus*) discovered in a princely tomb dating from the eighth century BC. Although the wheels are gone, its iron wheel protectors, attached to the wooden wheels by metal clamps, exist, along with bronze finial rings that covered the wheel hubs. Pieces of another more workaday cart (*carpentum*) were also found.

These were discovered intact in 1965 in the *Tomba dei Flabelli*, located a mile or so west of Trevignano in the neighborhood called Olivetello. At least one tomb wall,

Iron protecting rims for the wooden wheels of an Etruscan cart, Trevignano Civic Museum.

curiously to us today, had been painted red. Inside it was an elegantly decorated flat bronze *flabellum* ("fan" in Italian). A true *flabellum* or fan made of decorated flat bronze in the shape of a circle with a handle had been found in a tomb in nearby Etruscan Tarquinia—hence the name—but in this case it is a misnomer, for it is a rectangle made of decorated bronze in the shape of a big, flat trapezoid eighteen inches tall. Rather than a fan, this was a standard of honor which the chieftain would have held to demonstrate his importance during processions, political meetings and religious ceremonies.

Another indication of upper-crust Etruscan Trevignano is the skeleton of a chieftain. His status among his peers in the late eighth or early seventh century BC is clearly defined by the items buried with him in his tomb, discovered in 1987 on the hillside at Ricostano. His skeletal remains were not cleaned and polished, but kept intact and removed in a huge, single block. Almost six feet tall, he was originally called the "Etruscan warrior," for with his skeleton is a dagger and its sheath while on his knees is a shield of bronze, still at that time a status symbol despite the more mundane commercial passion for objects made of iron. Looking closely, the archaeologists who managed to remove the remains within its burial context also saw that, by his skull, was a bronze razor—for what purpose is unclear—and by his shoulder, a scepter. This scepter, together with shield and dagger, showed that he was not only a warrior, but also a chieftain. To travel into battle, in a triumphal parade or, perhaps, to the nearby hot springs in wintertime, the chieftain would have worn on his feet sandals and around his shoulders, a woolen cape; both sandals and bobbins from looms were also found.

Both *flabellum* and skeletal remains of the chieftain are on view in the museum along with the cart wheel guards, jewelry and myriad large and small glossy black baked ceramic pots, called "*bucchero*" ware. Typically Etruscan grave offerings (perhaps they held scents to cover the smell of death), the *bucchero* pots are low-cost imitations of bronze. *Bucchero* is believed to be a fusion of pottery worked by the earlier Villanovans, but influenced by the more advanced cultures of the eastern Mediterranean. Many of the objects found at Trevignano were obviously imports, but some were locally produced and show motifs from Syria, Lebanon and elsewhere in the eastern Mediterranean, as well as from Greece. Their orientalizing motifs include griffins, sphynxes, eagles, lotus blossoms, and the heads of gorgons, or monstrous females. On one outstanding vase, described as a nuptial pot, are depicted an eagle, a panther, a lion, a griffon, two sphynxes and a hare.

Several of the votive pots made of black *bucchero* sport tiny bas reliefs showing a woman tugging at her braids in grief. Suggesting a long-distance connection, this same theme of the woman in mourning who tugs at pigtails exists in an ivory version from the eastern Mediterranean, while in ancient Egypt's Tomb of Ramses mourning goddesses gaze down at the defunct while tugging at a long plait of hair they have pulled over their forehead. A number of pottery plates with holes that suggest they were hung from a wall were found in tombs just off Via della Macchia. As these artifacts show, during the four or five centuries of Etruscan power the town was fairly important in relation to the other nearby independent Etruscan miniature city-states with which it traded, thanks to its early roadway system, the fertility of the land and the water from the myriad hillside springs. From these the water was funneled, even then, into simple aqueducts which brought water toward fields needing irrigation in dry times and, in wet, drainage—more or less just as today.

7

Roman conquest

If you must break the law, do it to seize power.
In all other cases observe it.

—Julius Caesar

In 387 BC the Romans, as skilled at engineering as they were bellicose, besieged the important Etruscan city of Veii, which lies midway between Lake Bracciano and Rome. The brutal siege went on for no less than ten years. In the end Veii was conquered: the cunning Romans pretended to be continuing their siege of the walled town from the outside, while actually tunneling beneath it, to burst suddenly into the center of Veii, caught by surprise. From Veii the Romans continued northward to make other conquests. But before they could achieve those, they first had to build, for their soldiers, paved roads leading from Rome into the coveted territories. The most important road leading north, it became the Via Cassia, which led to Veii and then had to be continued northward. (It is still among the most important Roman roads.)

Trevignano was one of the Etruscan towns which answered to the far more powerful Veii. To reach it, Roman troops had to build another road that ran initially parallel to the Via Cassia, but then veered westward until it reached the northern shore of Lake Bracciano. This was the Via Clodia, and its construction around 225 BC brought the Roman troops to the lake; from it the Romans then moved onward to the seacoast. Vestiges of that ancient Roman road, running alongside the northern shore of Lake Bracciano, are visible at water's edge at km 17 between Trevignano and Bracciano.

In his Volume 6 of *The History of Rome,* Livy (Titus Livius, *c.* 60 BC– AD 17) relates that after that conquest of 387 BC the inhabitants of the Lacus Sabatinus territory were granted Roman citizenship. This "Tribus Sabatina" became one of twenty-two tribes defined as "rural" and accorded representation in the Roman Senate. The Romans' original road northward can be seen in the Tabula Peutingeriana, a map which shows the Via Cassia leading from Rome to Sabate, the lost Roman city. This map, whose sole surviving copy is in the National Library of Vienna, is believed to have been copied from a military map dating from the time of the Roman Empire. Its author was Corrado Peutinger (1465–1547), a humanist-archeologist from Bavaria.

Above: On distant hillside near Marcus Aurelius' villa, Vicarello palazzo with ancient Roman foundations.

Below: Tabula Peutingeriana segment shows the Via Cassia (horizontal green line) just above the ancient Roman city "Sabate". (*Photo Wikipedia Commons*)

When the Roman colonists arrived at Lake Bracciano, to those buildings that already existed in the Etruscan town they added their own. Upon the high hilltop overlooking today's Trevignano the Romans constructed a fort, built atop foundations of the earlier Etruscan fort. Vestiges of the Roman construction are visible even today amid the ruins of the later medieval fortress.

A reminder of the importance of the ancient Roman presence in Trevignano is the handsome marble temple architrave that lies, largely unnoticed, on the grass in the piazza facing town hall. In theory, the panel, one foot thick and 3 by 5 feet square, could have been brought to Trevignano from the emperor Marcus Aurelius's baths at Vicarello, but, if so, why transport it here? It is more likely that, like the Roman artifacts of marble inside the Trevignano civic museum, this stunning ancient panel is from Trevignano itself. One nineteenth century observer told of seeing, underwater off the Trevignano shore, ancient Roman ruins. Some are convinced that he is certain that "Roman ruins lie just under the piazza."

For now, the exact location of the Roman town as well as its Etruscan predecessor remains speculation. But that both existed is by now a certainty, as are the Roman vestiges inside the ruins of the medieval fortress, which we shall shortly visit.

The Romans were also present at Anguillara, where Roman matron Rutilia Polla ran a huge estate in the first century AD. Wealthy, she owned a sumptuous villa at a zone still called, after her, Pollina, on the lakefront abutting Trajan's Aqueduct midway between Trevignano and Anguillara. Her wealth came from owning a monopoly on the sale of fish to the Romans. Her contemporary, the illustrious jurist Proculus, wrote in his *Epistulae* that "Rutilila Polla emit lacum Sabatem Angularium"—that she had actually "bought the lake of Anguillara Sabatia."[22] Tradition holds that in the villa she also entertained military leaders who passed by *en route* to Rome.

It happened that the level of the lake rose, as it tended to do, and decreased Rutilia Polla's beachfront property by ten feet. She therefore sought help from Proculus, who is said to have practiced law under Nero, in making a claim to receive a compensatory stretch of inland territory. Proculus turned her down. He decreed that her ownership was limited to what had existed "at the moment of the contract.... She must not further extend her right of ownership by reason that the lake water later rose."[23] Not even rich Rutilia Polla could force the law into her favor.

At least a dozen aristocratic villas, and some believe that there were twice that many, were built during the grand period of ancient Rome and especially its sun-bathed northern shore, where two emperors had built their villas. Encircling Lake Bracciano (again, at that time Lacus Sabatina), these were others which, like Rutilia Polla's, were swallowed by the upsurging water. Vestiges of the foundations of some of these, plus other ancient Roman elements, can today be seen close to the shoreline, especially in the shadow of the Vicarello promontory. If little else is visible to date, it is because of the thick layer of sediment at the lake bottom. In the end, so we are told, the new Roman town came to be considered almost as important as Caere, today's Cerveteri, which lies on the seacoast. Water was and is power.

An early authoritative historian of Trevignano was Paolo Bondi da Fiumalbo, a priest-cum-archaeologist, whose *Memorie Storiche sulla Città Sabazia* was published in 1836. In it he wrote that, "It is certain that Trevignano already existed in the time when the Emperor Trajan constructed his celebrated Aqueduct... That fact [the aqueduct] makes this so evident that there is no reason to doubt it."

In main piazza, marble panel from unknown Roman temple.

In 1820 a farmer came upon a square piece of sarcophagus on our own Via della Macchia. It said that this was the tomb of Mida, beloved wife of "DMS Titicus"—Titus, her husband. "She merits this," said the inscription. Another in the town square dating from the third century AD honors Gavii Capitonis Maximiani, believed to have been a scribe. Ten years before this a uniquely important ancient Roman marble tombstone and sarcophagus were uncovered by a team of four oxen ploughing a field. "I saw the sarcophagus with my own eyes," wrote Bondi.[24] "Topping its cover [are] great big tiles, which defended it perfectly from any damage weather or time might bring." The sarcophagus was still half buried in the ground when its cover was pried open. The onlookers were stunned, Bondi recorded. "No sooner were the bones exposed to the open air, than they dissolved into minute bits of dust." The finders were also disappointed at there being no tomb offerings made of gold. Instead the sole object found inside the sarcophagus was a badly rusted sword. The tombstone, which Bondi described as "deeply corroded," survived, but exists only in part—fortunately, that part containing a dedication. Bondi's oxen hauled away the tombstone, which he placed in his own garden. That was in 1810, and years would pass before that dedication could be transcribed by Bondi's friend the architect Giacomo Palazzi. Seeking help for his translation, Palazzi had also consulted the erudite Antonio Nibby (1792–1839), a noted archaeologist who had worked on the original excavation of the Colosseum and co-authored a book on Rome with Sir William Gell of Pompeii fame.

D.M.
COVMBLAHAV
POLYAENUS ACI
OR - CONIUGI DULG
ISSIMAE ET INGO
IMPARABILI SUAE
VIXIT ANN. XXXIII M-
XI D- III- MEum V
EXIT ANNIS Vili iM.-
II- D- XV- BENEMER
ENTI FECI

With Nibby's help it was learned that the tombstone in Bondi's garden carried a dedication by Polyaenus to his "*coniugi dulcissimae et incomparabili*", his "very sweet and incomparable wife," who lived just 33 years, 11 months, 3 days, and "8 years, 2 months 15 days at my side." She "well merited" the monument, the mourning husband added.

That Polyaenus had lived in Trevignano was extraordinary news. The name is fairly unusual, and, with Nibby's help, Bondi and Palazzi agreed that this was the famous Polyaenus, a Greek historian born in Macedonia. After serving in the military, he came to Rome, where he worked as lawyer and magistrate, around the year 161 or at about the time when Marcus Aurelius co-ruled the empire with Lucius Verus. To these co-emperors Polyaenus dedicated a book in AD 163 which has gone down in history as one of the most unique works of ancient Rome, *Stratagems of War*. In its eight books, or chapters, Polyaenus analyzed no less than than nine hundred different strategies.

One of his comments in II of *Stratagems* gives an idea of his way of thinking: "Philip [of Macedon] once broke of his army command a man of rank from Taranto, because he took baths in warm water, saying: 'You seem a stranger to Macedonian customs, which do not indulge the use of warm water, even to a woman in child-birth.'" If this identification is correct, if the loving Polyaenus of the tombstone is the same as the tough Polyaenus of the *Stratagems of War*, how did this man, noteworthy in his own time, happen to come with his wife to Trevignano in the age of Marcus Aurelius? As it happened, between AD 162 and 165, these co-emperors were fighting a war against the Parthians in northeastern Iran. Polyaenus, who was by then about fifty years of age, was obviously too old to participate. After having worked as a lawyer in Rome, suggest Nibby and Bondi, Polyaenus had therefore been dispatched to Trebonianum. There is a logic to this: Vicus Aurelius, just down the road from Trevignano, belonged to Marcus Aurelius himself, the emperor to whom Polyaenus dedicated his book on war. The hot sulphur baths of Vicarello would have been just the right place for an aging warrior to find repose while its owner the emperor was on the warpath. Nevertheless authorities have ever since argued about this identification. One suggested that the grave marker is of a stone that seems to predate Polyaenus. To this others respond that people often reutilized older stones; any number of Christian tombstones show earlier evocations to classical deities. Definitive proof of his presence in Trevignano, which seems not unlikely, would kite the town of Trebonianum into a new level of importance among today's scholars of Roman antiquity.

8

Desperately seeking Sabatia

He who recalls and calls every evil borne
by him wear them forever

—Bracciano proverb

It was August of 2017, and the lake had undergone a nearly five-foot drop in its depth. This was exactly the opposite of what happened in the time of Rutilia Polla, when rising water shrank her beachfront property; now the receding water expanded the beach. People with metal detectors took this as an invitation to go hunting for gold rings and earrings lost by today's swimmers, but also to forage for metal coins and bits of jewelry from antiquity; one friend walking his dog on the beach happened upon two ancient Roman coins of bronze. Others rushed to collect bits and pieces of ancient carvings. Even a small bomb from the Second World War was found, a stone's throw from the beach area reserved for dogs. My own search was different, but based upon the same premise. Two years of studying Lake Bracciano had left me ever more fascinated with lost Sabatia. To date no definitive answer to the intriguing question of just where this unique ancient Roman city lay has been found. Could the receding water provide hints?

That an important Roman town named Sabatia existed on Lake Bracciano after the Romans conquered the lake territory around 273 BC seems to be a fact even though cautious scholars point out that only late Roman and medieval texts mention the town. However, the very fact that the lake was called Lacus Sabatinus suggests that the town did exist by the lake in the pre-Christian centuries.

Some historical evidence comes from Sosigenes of Alexandria, a Greek astronomer and mathematician in the employ of Julius Caesar, writing late in the 1st century BC, or at least a century after the town disappeared because of an earthquake or a sudden rise in the water. Although in his time the town of Sabatia had already been lost, Sosigenes reported that deep underwater in Lacus Sabatinus temples, a stretch of wall and some statues as well were visible. "The inhabitants of the place say that a city was once here," he wrote in his *Geography*—here, but just where, he did not or could not say.

Although today's Trevignano has existed only since the twelfth century, in recent decades local fishermen, like those recorded by Sosigenes, reported spotting traces of ancient wall, deep underwater in the lake just in front of Trevignano.

As lake shrank in 2017, mounds of stone—possibly ancient Roman burial markers—suddenly became visible. Today all stones are scattered.

That ghostly vision is an echo of what the eminent priest-historian Paolo Bondi da Fiumalbo wrote in his *Memorie storiche sulla città Sabazia ora Lago Sabatino* in 1836: that on a morning after a horrendous storm, a woman walked down to the shore at Trevignano in hopes of finding one of the big fish that rough waters sometimes deposited there. Instead she suddenly saw, not a real fish, but a statuette of a fish made of gold. Ingenuously, she took this golden fish to the *vice-Principe* or deputy mayor of Trevignano (at the time a Vatican property), who repaid her with a few lire. Alas that was the last ever seen of the golden fish.

Recalling another local legend, Bondi wrote that a storm had once tossed on to the beach a small statue carved of rare porphyry. It showed two figures: Ganymede, the mythical hero of Troy, serving wine on a tray to the god Zeus. Like the golden fish, this too has disappeared.

From its vast number of ancient Etruscan tombs, Bondi deduced that the Etruscan city was large and important. With the Roman conquest, he wrote, the town continued to exist, albeit with both its politics and its population altered by the colonies arriving from Rome. As further evidence that Sabatia lay on the north, or Trevignano, shore of the lake Bondi pointed to the proximity of the hot springs at Vicarello and to the existence of the Roman road that lay alongside the north shore of the lake. What is certain, he declared, "is that Trevignano already existed at the time when the Emperor Trajan constructed his celebrated Aqueduct.... There can be no doubt about it."

Bondi's conclusion: "It is not difficult for me to conjecture, with some certainty, that the sole town that escaped, following the destruction and natural reordering and recomposition of the land, could only be our Trevignano.... the most ancient, most beautiful, powerful and wealthy city of its time." It was his conviction, he wrote, that even before the definitive destruction of Sabatia, an earlier earthquake had damaged the city, leaving "a few ruins of buildings buried beneath the waters."

The territory is indeed subject to earthquakes, and to sudden dramatic rises in the water level. In the Neolithic period, the level of the lake water rose suddenly and drastically, as we have seen at La Marmotta; the same happened later to some of the aristocratic villas built in the time of the Emperor Marcus Aurelius on the shoreline of Lake Bracciano. At least a century after Sabatia disappeared these were similarly if not as deeply swallowed; remnants of the foundations of some, plus other ancient Roman elements like a mill wheel and a statue base, are visible today just underwater and even at shoreline. It is important to recall that those villas were built at least a century after Sabatia disappeared.

As times change, so does the lake. In 2017 the level of the lake water fell by at least five feet for the first time in literally millennia. With the receding water and expanded beach, piles of stones were suddenly revealed for the first time in centuries. Walking along the newly broadened lake shore I photographed areas where scattered stones were concentrated for about one mile; on either side of this newly expanded beach the waterfront was entirely devoid of the piled-up stones. At sight of this I had the thrilling sense that I had found Sabatia.

Some were plainly worked stones, all of crude local tuff rock. Disappointingly, I found no trace of marble; if there, it had already been illegally carted away by beachcombers. However, in various places the stones appeared to form a line, as if from a collapsed wall. Here and there were rounded tubes as if once part of a column; the action of the water could hardly, of itself, carve columns. Most interesting of all were mounds of stones. When she was shown my photograph of these dozens of mounds on the newly visible beach, archaeologist Dora Cirone, who has worked for thirty years in the Roman Forum, suggested that they may be burial mounds—that is, burials just outside the wall of the complex, which I take to be the upper level of lost Sabatia. It will be up to the archaeologists to study these mounds as well as the stones that seem to take the shape of columns, and the other stones that appear to have been worked by man.

In hopes of finding a definitive answer for the whereabouts of Sabatia, in 1982 the Swiss oceanographer Jacques Piccard, son of the inventor Auguste Piccard, was invited to explore underwater Lake Bracciano.

Descending over five hundred feet deep inside his bathyscaphe, the "F. A. Forel," Piccard spent seventy-five underwater hours that August in his search for traces of the literally deep past. He reported finding evidence of five submerged ancient villages on stilts, subsequently identified as dating from the Bronze Age, as he related at a press conference held inside the Castle of Bracciano. At the same press conference he confirmed on the basis of water samples that the lake water was not polluted, even in the vicinity of the trio of lake towns.

When local fishermen begged him to explain why, at a certain point, their nets were torn, he suggested that sharp rocks were the cause. He also discovered the carcass of a four-engine airplane lost in the lake back in 1977. However, to the disappointment of many, he reported finding no indication of where the famous lost Roman town of Sabatia lay. Perhaps, as some have suggested, the vestiges of Sabatia are covered by a thick layer of mud, making the ruins invisible. This, of course, is exactly why the Neolithic village known as La Marmotta was undiscovered for thousands of years beneath 9 feet of mud and 24 feet of water, or until workmen laying a new aqueduct happened to trawl straight through it in the 1980s, as described in chapter 6, "Bread and Wine". Nevertheless, as Piccard privately confided to Ofelio Maciucchi, Trevignano's foremost Twentieth century town historian, he was personally convinced that the ruins of Sabatia lie just in front of today's Trevignano.[25]

9

Aqueductors

If for Saint Bibiana rain comes forth,
For a month and a week it will pour

—Bracciano proverb

In the course of two decades I had stood countless times near the bus stop on the main drag through Trevignano, often to buy bread at Stefanelli's bakery kitty-corner across the street. It was only when I chanced to meet Michael and Edward O'Neill, the British father–son team known as the "Aqueduct Hunters" that I learned what lay behind, or rather above, that very banal bus stop: a stretch of ancient Roman aqueduct. It had been built under the Emperor Trajan (AD 98–117), and inaugurated on June 24 of AD 109, when Rome was home to 1.25 million thirsty citizens. How, I wondered, had I been so ingenuous as not to realize that this was more than an old wall?

Michael and Edward were more knowledgeable. Michael ("Mike") first visited Rome in 1996. Moving here permanently in 2002, he founded MEON HDTV Productions six years later, with the goal of using high definition film to document Roman archaeological treasures, and in particular its aqueducts. His documentary film-maker son and partner is Edward ("Ted"), the equally passionate aqueductor, as I thought of them. Ted, who has worked for the BBC and for the Italian TV broadcaster Mediaset, has also been an actor and is a fan of the classical theater, from Shakespeare and Molière to Tennessee Williams.

"With my son we have been researching and studying the Roman aqueducts for years," Mike told me one summer morning as he, Ted and I lingered over coffee at an outdoor table at Ermete's Café in the piazza. "The citizens of ancient Rome had an abundance of water from the aqueducts, which permitted both the population of the city and the Roman Empire as well to expand. Through the miraculous engineering of their water supplies, what are now ancient ruins had a huge influence on modern European civilization as well as on Rome.

"Our aim is to find the lost secrets of how this came about—the clean drinking water, the latrines, the laundries, the splendid public baths, the water mills powered by aqueduct water."

Like many other ancient Roman towns, Trebonianum (that is, Trevignano), was served by primitive aqueducts built by the Etruscans who preceded the Romans, and

Below Vicarello promontory, arches of Trajan's Aqueduct, restored by Pope Paul V. (*Photo courtesy David Willey*)

perhaps even before them; we know that a Bronze Age village lies under the lake waters at Vicarello and probably one underwater in front of Trevignano.

At several points on our own steep street, Via della Macchia, which is scattered with underground Etruscan tombs (at least two near our house), spring water occasionally still gushes its way across the road, and in 2001 archaeologists discovered an underground gallery for an impressive Etruscan aqueduct. This "*cunicolo ipogeo*", or buried water channel, had been dug through the soft tuff stone of our hillside; inside it measured 8½ feet tall by almost 28" wide (2.60 m by 70 cm), making it large enough for a person to walk through. The "gallery," as its excavator, Roberto Manigrasso calls it, was partially collapsed, either because the terrain was uneven or because of clandestine excavating for booty. Despite the cave-in, archaeologists report that this invisible underground Etruscan aqueduct gallery is nevertheless "rather well preserved."

Given its resemblance to pre-Roman aqueducts, including those at the nearby important Etruscan cities of Caere and Veio, this one presumably dates from between the sixth and fourth centuries BC.[26] Its construction was complex and required skilled engineering and abundant unskilled laborers. Another Etruscan aqueduct, which later channeled water toward and into that built by the Roman Emperor Trajan at Vicarello, lies a few yards further above that Trevignano bus stop. And adjacent to Trajan's at the bottom of the road is a fountain called the Fontana San Martino, still in daily use. Inside that fountain, which connects just across the road to Trajan's Aqueduct (in Italian, the *Aqua Traiana*), archaeologists discovered Etruscan pottery fragments which far predate Trajan and ancient Rome. This was not a great town, but such evidence of Etruscan life—the tombs and aqueducts that underlie Trevignano—speak to us not only

has suggested this was a state project because Rome, densely populated, was shifting in that period from handouts of grain to the distribution of baked bread, and therefore required grain already ground; in the mill-race remains coins were found suggesting that private citizens purchased the flour.[31]

From that position on the Janiculum Hill the water that had arrived from the springs above Lake Bracciano finally descended into the city, to deliver water for the first time to those living in the Transtiberina, today's Trastevere quarter. Until that time a small earlier aqueduct, the Alseatino, built by the emperor Augustus, had brought water into the area, but scarcely enough to fill a small pond and to water a few orchards.

From Trastevere, Trajan's aqueduct crossed the Tiber River either via underwater pipes or a stone bridge; no one knows which. It is known, however, that the water arrived in central Rome, to the point where it provided abundant water for Trajan's "Naumachia" pond, near what would become the Vatican. There, in what burnished the emperor's image, spectators were entertained by mock naval battles. His naval battle pond, far smaller than that at the Colosseum, was inaugurated in the year 109. All told, until the sack of Rome in AD 410, the eleven aqueducts including Trajan's fed 1,212 public fountains and eleven imperial baths.

But a series of barbarian invasions wreaked havoc. In AD 537 the Goths cut the aqueducts. Further damage came after 567, when Germanic Longobard (Lombard) soldiers opposed to the Byzantine rulers in Rome battled their way down the Italian peninsula. Famous for their cruelty, theirs was a hodgepodge army said to be of 100,000 soldiers (one historian says 400,000) from various distant tribes—Bulgars, Ostrogoths, Saxons, Thuringians and others.

In 591, they conducted their second assault on the Italian peninsula. Bludgeoning their way toward Rome on the Via Cassia, they passed through Orvieto, Bagnoregio, Viterbo and then the castle town of Sutri, seven miles north of Trevignano. Their leader and most successful king at that time was Liutprand (690 - *c.*744), born of an originally German family in Pavia, then the Longobard capital. Sutri was in a particularly excellent position to guard the Via Cassia, but Liutprand prevailed. He was a Catholic, and subsequently, supposedly in hopes of pleasing the Pope, he withdrew from Sutri, but only after seriously damaging Trajan's aqueduct as it snaked in its half-circle around the lake. His soldiers also trashed the towns through which the aqueduct passed, including Trevignano.

At the Vicarello promontory with its hot springs three miles west of Trevignano, they destroyed what remained of the huge estate of Marcus Aurelius and ravaged the Roman villas lining the northern shore of the lake a few miles further west. Near the shore below the Vicarello baths, they also ravaged the ancient Roman market town, the Forum Clodii. As a result of that destruction, the exact location of the Forum Clodii is still a matter for conjecture.

Over two hundred years would pass before the Lombards were at last defeated by Charlemagne. Their presence has survived in Sutri, however, in the name of a Via Cassia restaurant, Liutprando. (Lombard power also survives in the name of the region surrounding Milan, Lombardia.)

The damages to Trajan's aqueduct were never repaired until, in the 1500s, the Renaissance was in full sway. Rome was wealthy once more, and its population was soaring due to immigration. As a result, pure water was running short, and successive pontiffs began to consider repairing the old Roman aqueducts. On Christmas Eve of 1580, Cardinal Giovanni Francesco Commendone and a fellow cardinal were dispatched to Lake Bracciano to study the sources of Trajan's ruined aqueduct to consider the feasibility of restoration. Their decision was that to do so was far too costly. Instead they elected to restore two old aqueducts lying east of Rome, the Aqua Vergine and the Alessandrino. However, especially for the Vatican, this was basically useless, for, as we have seen, these distant and older aqueducts delivered water onto a physically lower level. The pressure from these low-lying aqueducts did not suffice to send water to the Vatican or to Trastevere across the Tiber. Seeing a solution, Camillo Borghese, elected as Pope Paul V in 1605, purchased from Virginio Orsini, the duke of Bracciano, many of the ancient conduits and hillside springs to the north on Lake Bracciano that had carried water into the old aqueduct. To pay for the purchase, among other things he levied a tax upon the sale of wine.

Venetian engineer–medical doctor and inventor Giovanni Fontana began repairing the old aqueduct. Work was completed in 1608 at a cost of 400,000 scudi, and Trajan's aqueduct was reopened in 1612 with a magnificent display of water spurting into a monumental fountain in St. Peter's Square. This fountain, dating from 1490, had been expanded a decade later with the addition of a basin for watering horses. In 1612 Carlo Maderno cleverly redesigned and expanded it, to the point that tiny drops of water, driven by the power of gravity, rose in a delicate spray into the air, a *jet d'eau* created with the use of minimal water.

Still, the amount of water arriving through that now expensively renovated aqueduct continued to have a decidedly lower yield than in Trajan's time. With the dawn of the Baroque era and the Counter-Reformation, Roman pontiffs sought prestige through elaborate building programs, which included construction of new fountains.

Half a century after Maderno's fountain, Pope Clement X commissioned construction of a new fountain in St. Peter's Square. It was to be a replica of the first, built in 1490 and fed by water from the Aqua Traiana. These were the 1650s, and to add a second fountain required an additional supply of water. To analyze how to increase the water flow into St. Peter's Square, in 1657, the pope appointed the engineer–architect Luigi Bernini (1612–1681) his official "Architect of Waters". The younger brother of the more famous Gian Lorenzo Bernini, Luigi had deep experience: it was he who would raise the gigantic, heavy ancient Egyptian obelisk atop the finished Four Rivers Fountain in Piazza Navona when completed by his architect–sculptor brother.

Luigi grasped that the reason for the limited amount of water arriving was that the crucial and particularly abundant source by Lake Bracciano, beneath the church of Santa Fiora, had been omitted from the original purchase deal and still belonged to the descendants of the powerful Duke Paolo Giordano Orsini I (1541–1585). In his report of February 25, 1667, Luigi explained that beneath Santa Fiora was "the principal [source] of the whole antique Traianic Aqueduct.... In front of the church are the remains of connections, tanks, and pieces of conduit above and below where it flows out to drive the grain mills." *Grain mills*: Santa Fiora had been excluded from the costly papal purchase of the aqueduct tracts in 1605 because the particularly abundant Santa Fiora water source turned the wheel for, among others, the great Orsini-owned grain mill at Vigna Grande, which ground the flour for Bracciano bread. In addition, part of the original deal negotiated under Pope Paul V had been that, when completed, the Orsini family palazzi in Rome at Campo de' Fiori and at Monte Giordano would receive water for free.

The territory near Bracciano was owned by Paolo Giordano Orsini II, the duke of Bracciano, who lived there in its castle. He was the grandson of Paolo Giordano Orsini I, who had been educated at the courts of the Medici, the Farnesi and the Sforza, and was a patron of the arts, but also a notoriously nasty piece of goods. After marriage to the beautiful Isabella de' Medici, the daughter of Cosimo I, the two had lived (she only briefly, however) in the Bracciano Castle. Supposedly infuriated by her having an affair, he is said to have had her strangled in his presence, not at Bracciano, but in a Medici villa near Florence. (We shall return to this in chapter 10.)

Despite the omission of the Santa Fiora water, Luigi Bernini became convinced that the amount of water arriving from Trajan's aqueduct could be doubled. To compensate for the lack of those springs still owned by the Orsini, he suggested that water be drawn from the lake and, via a tube, connected to the aqueduct near Anguillara and hence sent on to Rome. Thanks to this added vein of Lake Bracciano water, when completed the improved aqueduct sent some 80,000 cubic meters of water into Trastevere and, through eight giant pipes crossing the Ponte Sisto Bridge, into Rome. But then a tough problem arose. Because it was taken directly from the lake, the water, now called the Acqua Paola for the pope, was no longer as pure as it had been when the aqueduct bore solely spring water. Romans called the new water foul, and engineer Luigi Bernini's "improvement" gave birth to a sarcastic local Roman expression: to say that something was "as good as the Acqua Paola" meant that it was simply bad.

In 1752 under Pope Benedict XIV the situation had not improved. An architect sent to examine the walls controlling the emissions of water into the aqueduct near Lake Bracciano described them as "broken and not diligently maintained," and hence insufficient to bring the amount required into Rome.[32] On the other hand, at times so much water rushed into the aqueduct that the cumulative effect was to damage fountains, bridges, fields and orchards, said a document found in the archives of Anguillara. In addition there was uncertainty as to who was to maintain the aqueduct.

The problems continued. During the Second World War, a stretch of Trajan's aqueduct at Trevignano was destroyed by being bombed by retreating German soldiers shortly before the arrival of the Allied troops, according to historian Maciucchi.[33]

Nevertheless today the aqueduct remains in vital function and continues to serve the city of Rome and, because the water passes through the papal state, the Vatican also.

As for the drinking water, the citizens now living on or near the lake are advised to avoid drinking their tap water because it is laced with arsenic, albeit in an apparently small amount. They must either purchase mineral water, which is usually bottled in plastic. Trevignano citizens can fill their own bottles with purified water, free of charge, from a tap in the center of the village parking lot, my choice.

10

Fortress

The procession re-enters
from where it takes leave

—Bracciano proverb

The BBC likes to warn viewers that some images it is about to show will be disturbing. Well, to write about feudalism is potentially disturbing. Those who bore easily should skip to the next even though they will not understand what has made Trevignano what it is and why.

Some six thousand of Italy's rural villages—the *borghi*—have been reduced to ghost towns. Life there simply became too difficult. Even though tourists are rediscovering the *borghi*, most houses and schools have been deserted; fields left fallow, and shops shuttered. Earthquakes struck all too often, so that families had to flee to safety. One lovely mountaintop *borgo,* Codera near Sondrio, is intact, but has no road access; its few residents commute by helicopter.

Something similar happened elsewhere, of course. But, as journalist Deborah Needleman of *The New York Times* points out, what makes this particularly sad in Italy is "the exquisite architectural character of its hill towns, as well as the quality of the handiwork and traditions that were born, cultivated and perfected here. These towns and their craftsmanship are what we think of when we think of Italy—as fundamental to the country's identity as its important cities and grand artistic legacies."[34]

The good news is that *borgo* tourism throughout Italy is on the rise, especially among those already familiar with Rome and Florence and wary of the new mass tourism. Little Trevignano's is among those suddenly discovered. Unlike many, Trevignano's tiny *borgo*, half on a hill, half by the shore, never became a ghost town. Although sacked by barbarians of various stripes, its walled *borgo* is as alive and well as when built in the Middle Ages. Its single narrow main street just 150 yards long—that street down which the blind postman Giuseppe Vincola found his daily way a century ago—still slices through the *borgo* from end to end. Twin gates originally stood at either end of the little street, both with stout wooden doors locked by night and whenever danger loomed, as it tended to do.

Inside the *borgo* are short alleys and miniscule lanes, some running uphill, to weave around the Renaissance-era church. Houses are rarely more than two or three stories tall.

The foundations of one of these twin round towers at lake shore were apparently undermined by wild waves and earthquakes, and at some point crumbled into the lake—or perhaps was sacrificed in 1798 to facilitate the passage of farm carts carrying produce to markets at Anguillara. Fortunately the other watch tower still exists today at Trevignano, at waterfront just off the main piazza, where it nestles almost invisibly between a café and a restaurant.

During this period of the militarization of Trevignano the territory was fairly prosperous. Among other things, Trevignano's neighbor Sutri featured prominently on the pilgrims' (and merchants') walk toward Rome on the so-called Via Francigena, which included the Via Cassia. Pilgrims needed to eat and to sleep, and so, along with the Sutri shoemakers, taverns prospered. In the thirteenth or fourteenth century a Roman-era Mithreum had been converted into a Christian church, the Madonna del Parto, and on one wall a fresco depicts a file of these pilgrims walking toward Rome. (Sutri is still a Via Francigena destination, and pilgrims walking through Sutri, including in groups, remain a common sight.) Some chose, and still choose, to walk toward Rome through Trevignano.

As fortunes shifted, once again the Di Vico managed to own the Trevignano fortress and *borgo*. But the Di Vico gradually lost control over it, and in 1377 Rome itself desired Trevignano with its fortress. Lacking the funds to buy it, the Roman Senate borrowed a substantial sum of money from Latino Orsini. As a guarantee for that loan, the Senate gave him Trevignano with its fortress. This pawnshop treatment of Trevignano paved the way for the Orsini to wrest control over the entire lake territory. And in fact in just a decade, the last Di Vico, Francesco, who had reoccupied the Trevignano fortress with his army, was murdered, ending their reign.

The Orsini were one of the oldest and mightiest of the Roman families; altogether they would produce three popes and thirty-four cardinals. They came to own 126 castles scattered hither and yon between Tuscany further north and Apulia in the south, but for two centuries the Bracciano castle was their stronghold and heart of Orsini power. By 1414, two decades after the last Di Vico was murdered, the Orsini owned all the lake towns: Castrum Brasani (Bracciano), Castrum Trivingiani, Castrum Vicarelli, and Castrum Anguillariae. As Orsini ambitions grew, so did the improvements in their castle. By the late 1400s its original medieval tower was surrounded with stout walls, entered via two drawbridges. Along with the castle the Bracciano *borgo* too grew, and the town acquired its own aqueduct, paper mill, tapestry workshop and ironmongery. Sported everywhere was the Orsini crest, featuring a rose and a bear; the latter was a play on words since *orso* is Italian for bear.

Curiously, the Orsini were at least for a time indifferent to the lake itself. Leonardo Buti, a Roman nobleman, controlled the fishing industry, some of whose profits went to the Church of Santa Maria in Trastevere.[36]

Since the Middle Ages the Colonna had been the enemies of the Orsini, but times were changing and new enemies appeared. The same year America was discovered, a conclave elected Pope Alexander VI, born Rodrigo de Borgia near Valencia in Spain. In 1496 Giovanni Borgia, aided and abetted by his (presumed) father the pope, launched an attack against the Orsini. Helping Giovanni Borgia were troops provided by the Colonna and the duke of Urbino.

Before attacking the giant, well defended Bracciano castle, Borgia first set siege to Anguillara, which caved in fairly rapidly. From across the lake Trevignano then came

Immense fifteenth-century Orsini-Odescalchi Castle dominates city of Bracciano.

under attack by boat. Trevignano resisted, and, when his siege failed, Giovanni Borgia returned, trying a new tack, by land. Technological developments had made cannon smaller and more mobile. From a hilltop directly across from the fortress on Monte Rocca Romana, the Borgia army fired from a newly developed cannon, whose reach was farther than any in the past. This unexpected attack left the fortress gravely damaged, to the point that Trevignano's "Rocca" became useless and had to be completely abandoned in 1525. In the meantime Borgia had managed to seize a vast array of Orsini properties—but not Bracciano, where they were defeated. After their war with the Borgias ended, and upon the death of their family pope, the Orsini reclaimed their properties including Trevignano. The stout defense of its fortress helped the Orsini win the battle at the Bracciano castle, and in the early years of the sixteenth century, the Orsini built the church above the Trevignano *borgo*, in thanksgiving.

Despite having been sacked and seriously damaged, and now without its fortress, its *borgo* remained fairly intact. A few projects to rebuild it were made, but Trevignano's fort never recovered, and today still lies in precarious ruins. Its lone watch tower survived until lightning destroyed it after the year 1900.

Ironically, in coming centuries the destruction of the Trevignano fortress, while curtailing the strategic importance of the town, had the advantage of leaving its people to live in peace. Trevignano had its own resources, its pastures and the lake. Its

Young Cosimo was the first of his tribe to deign to visit Trevignano, hitherto known solely to the administrators who collected the income from the five-square-mile family *feudo* (and doubtlessly held back a portion for themselves). Cosimo, who became a friend and patron to the era's historian, the priest Don Bondi, was generous: it was he who allowed the townspeople's cattle and sheep to graze once more on feudal pasturelands that had previously been off limits. On the wooded hillside on the Rocca Romana (today publicly-owned parkland) he permitted the locals to collect firewood on what had been off limits.

The newcomers from Tuscany taught the local farmers innovative agricultural techniques, and a few married and remained to live in Trevignano. With them the Tuscan agriculturists brought improvements to the customary harvests of hemp, wheat, wine, olive oil, fruit and potatoes, and also introduced the exotic (and well paid) cultivation of mulberries. A previous town owner had introduced silk worms, and Cosimo expanded upon this, bringing about the profitable production of silk.

At the outset this new feudal owner of Trevignano despised the local populace, whom he initially described in his diary as "*miserabile, cattiva e pigra*"—miserable, bad and lazy. But after becoming personally acquainted with the townspeople, Cosimo set aside his initial hostility. In a printed pamphlet he praised them as good workers, serious and full of initiative. That pamphlet, "Considerazioni: L'Agricultura di Trevignano," was dedicated to Cardinal Giacomo Giustiniani, "beneficent protector of the earth." He improved roads; one was our own twisting Via della Macchia, which from rustic footpath on the lower slope of the Rocca Romana became a trail accessible to farm carts. He drained Le Pantane, the swampland on Trevignano's outskirts, in 1836. No one yet knew what caused malaria, but draining that swamp surely reduced its victims in the town.

Because of a fire, parish records were lost between 1804 and 1866. Still, a degree of prosperity had obviously arrived under Cosimo, for the number of families in the *borgo* surged, as did the number of children per family. Whereas at the end of the eighteenth century families had no more than three or four children, by the 1820s the norm had risen to eight or nine children

In Cosimo's day, four out of five in the town could neither read nor write. To combat this illiteracy, he coaxed a local priest into opening an elementary school which girls as well as boys could attend for the first time. All children, said a clause in what amounted to a sharecropping contract, were to be taught "to read and to count." During the famine year of 1846, when the townspeople appealed to Cosimo for help, he distributed free grain "including to day laborers" (*braccianti*). The entire economy improved, as another increase in the town population testifies; by then five hundred souls were living there, two hundred more than in 1774. Cosimo's contributions were widely recognized. The success did not go unnoticed, and in 1835 Pope Gregory XVI elevated Trevignano to a princedom "in perpetuity." In 1847 Domenico De Crollis, a Roman doctor and poet, dedicated a book of sonnets to Cosimo in praise of his philanthropy and experiments in agriculture at Trevignano.

After four decades of management by Cosimo, Trevignano, which was still a papal state, passed into the hands of Prince Alessandro di Torlonia in 1854. Famously known as the "Pope's banker" because he came from the banking family that administered Vatican finances, Torlonia was a patron of the arts, and married into the aristocratic Colonna family; an ancestor Giovanni Torlonia had been made the duke of Bracciano by Pope

The "Pope's banker" Prince Alessandro di Torlonia acquired Trevignano in 1854.

Pius VI back in 1794. By comparison with most of the others in the centuries of feudal ownership of Trevignano, Alessandro di Torlonia was an interesting figure and modern thinker. In one extraordinary exploit, shortly before acquiring Trevignano he had utilized his own money in an effort to reclaim Lake Fucino in the Abruzzo, a gigantic project. However, some historians accuse him of taking advantage of the generalized poverty in the Roman countryside by snatching up properties on the cheap, including but not only Trevignano. In addition, Cosimo Conti was a hard act to follow, so popular for many decades that even after Torlonia took over, Cosimo, not Torlonia, was widely known as the "Prince of Trevignano." Just eight years after snapping up Trevignano, Torlonia decided that his *feudo* did not earn him enough money, so he passed it on to Gino Ginori Conti, a relative of the previous. But this Conti restoration did not last long.

Curiously, unification of Italy after 1870 did little to alter the relationship between the farm workers of Trevignano and their feudal lords and masters. With unification Trevignano was no longer part of the pontifical state, but of the new Italy. Although the number of inhabitants rose to 749, the conditions of "misery" worsened after Italian unification because of that brutal law of 1888 that limited the peasant farmers' rights to cut wood, let their flocks into the pastures and even sow seeds—rights which had been acquired only by dint of centuries of struggle against feudal lords.[40]

In 1880 Trevignano was resold to the Del Drago, yet another titled family which had already had a stake in the *feudo*. Filippo Del Drago was the prince of Fucino, the lake area in the Abruzzo. During the Del Drago administration a Trevignano farmer's work day lasted twelve hours, and for miserable pay, just 1 lire 20 cents for skilled workers, 90 cents for the unskilled. Feudal law required farmers to hand over one-sixth of the grape harvest and fishermen, one-quarter of every catch. In theory feudal privileges no longer existed, but Prince Filippo Del Drago ignored this, and persisted in claiming them nevertheless. Not surprisingly, he became immensely unpopular, "a feudal lord... exploiting the local people even though, after unification of Italy, feudal privilege no longer existed."[41] Del Drago's insistence upon enjoying feudal privileges was nothing new: the aristocrats who had for centuries owned the town and its land—the Curtabraca, Di Vico, Orsini, Grillo, Cosimo Conti, Torlonia—had all obliged the fishermen, shepherds and farmers working the soil to hand over a huge percentage of their catch and crops on the basis of a feudal edict dating from 1320 if not before. Town historian Maciucchi lists the families who suffered most under the harsh Del Drago regime: Bui, Simeoni, Giuliani and Avincola, all residents of Trevignano since the early 1700s; we shall meet today's Avincola family descendants in the chapter "Café Society." In fact, some of those ancient feudal privileges survived right into the 1950s, as we shall see.

Shortly after Italian unification in 1870, Trevignano's public elementary school was for boys and girls between six and nine years of age (the first such school dated from the 1830s). Early in the school year, classrooms were full, but as the months passed the children were needed to work in the fields, and classrooms gradually emptied. As a result, the "desired effect" was lacking, wrote the Minister of Public Education in a letter of 1887. This lack was caused, he wrote, by "the harsh life [*angustia*] and poverty, the families' misery and ignorance, laziness and sloppiness, and lack of help from the authorities." Still, he said, ending on a positive note, this could be overcome by teachers willing to encourage those "admirable virtues" which schooling provides. Indeed, just two years later a school for illiterate adults, which at that time meant anyone over the age of twelve, was also established in Trevignano. Classes were held evenings and on holidays. From Rome came a promise that if a class achieved more than fifteen students, Rome itself would pay for the teacher. Nazzareno Rocchi of Trevignano became one of those teachers, and also set up a circulating library, graced with thirty-eight books.

Another elementary school teacher in Trevignano was Gaetano Garafini. Seeking a boost in his wages, in the 1880s Garafini sent a 72-line rhyming letter to the *Podestà*. This medieval title derived from the Latin word for power, *potestas*, and in Garafini's time meant more or less the power-that-be, a combination of magistrate and mayor. Garafini's letter began:

> Mi danno sol quindici lire al mese
> Per il servizio, che le presto in scuola;
> Con questo poi, ho da sostener le spese,
> Alla moglie, tre maschi, e una figliuola....

Which translates more or less to:

> Barely lire fifteen a month they give me
> For the service to the school I provide;
> With only this I must somehow feed
> Three boys, a girl and my bride.

Some of his early students were the children of shepherds from distant parts. During the early years after Italian unification shepherds from the mountains of Umbria, Abruzzo and the Marches, driven from their homes by the winter cold and seeking warmth, arrived regularly with their flocks. This was the traditional transhumance, and before entering the town of Trevignano, these wandering shepherds had to pass through a customs station at Settevene along the road linking to the Via Cassia. Once in Trevignano, the shepherds and their flocks were made welcome. The sheep would be let into the lake to drink before being herded into a pen, built specifically for them near the clock tower entry into the *borgo*. Nearby was a fountain customarily used for washing wine kegs and for watering horses and donkeys. In that period the women were normally not allowed outside the *borgo* save to do the laundry in that fountain. "Italy is such a delightful place to live if you happen to be a man," muses Lilia, heroine of British author E. M. Forster's first novel, written in 1905, *Where Angels Fear to Tread*. Lilia was a widow who later married a local Italian. As Forster points out in the novel, set in San Gimignano in Tuscany, which he calls Monteriano, women in Italy do not leave their houses much, for to walk is not genteel. "In the democracy of the café or the street the great question of our life has been solved, and the brotherhood of man is a reality. But it is accomplished at the expense of the sisterhood of women.... They have, of course, their house and their church.... It is all very sad." Nevertheless, in Trevignano when shepherds were washing their flocks on the little beach just outside the *borgo*, they might encounter some of the women, hard at work scrubbing their linens and hanging them out to dry on bushes. The result: some shepherds married and remained in Trevignano. Nor were these the only love affairs with outsiders. The Carabinieri national paramilitary corps had been created back in 1814 with the dual responsibility of maintaining public order and defending the state, which at that time meant Piedmont and Sardinia. Little more than a decade after the unification of Italy, a Carabinieri brigadier and his four men assigned to Trevignano occupied office space in a fairly new palazzo (now the town hall) built just outside the *borgo* a few steps from the clock tower. After Vittorio Squarzolo, one of the Carabinieri, fell in love with a local lass, Maria Franchini, and married her, the couple produced eight children, whose ten descendants would become themselves Carabinieri. It did not end there. Vittorio had a Carabinieri friend from Pavia, who visited Trevignano, married Maria's sister, Michelina, and produced four children.

During a marriage ceremony, the groom would first walk to the bride's home to collect her, then with family members walk proudly through the *borgo* as villagers tossed at them flower petals, rice and small change. The brides were too poor to have white wedding gowns and so were married in colored frocks. Poverty also meant no honeymoon, but there would be a feast with dancing, and, after that, perhaps a little ride in a cart drawn by a donkey. Ironically, today's Trevignano town hall and its churches are extraordinarily popular venues for weddings, including of distant outsiders, and brides and grooms are photographed on the beach. Semblances of the old male–female social arrangements can sometimes still be seen in the town, however. Even in chilly weather older women sit nattering outdoors on the stone benches at street side while their mates, the older men, congregate in the cafés and on the park benches outside the *borgo* walls, with no female presence. As for today's young ladies, they are regularly out jogging and in the cafés, and not only there to work behind a shop counter.

By the late nineteenth century, thanks to improvements in the Italian economy, the population of Trevignano had quadrupled, reaching 1,024 inhabitants in 1900. That year the first four shops were opened in the *borgo*. One, a *merceria*, sold thread, cloth and buttons. Two sold food, another first for Trevignano; until that time Trevignanesi had to travel on horseback or by boat to Bracciano to buy household utensils and whatever food they could not produce or purchase at home. By 1920, the population had risen to over 1,500. The local priest, still responsible for the census, took the trouble to list everyone's job, thus providing an x-ray of the town's social structure at the end of the First World War. That year, 157 were farm workers ("*campagnolo*"). Although the Del Drago still owned vast holdings, twenty-seven other families were officially recognized as landowners, meaning they owned at least 10 hectares (25 acres) and twenty bovine animals. Ten more farmers worked their own orchards, another ten drove mules or oxen, six were shepherds, six made shoes, four were tailors or seamstresses, three were carpenters, two delivered mail, two were blacksmiths and nine were fishermen. Lastly, there was one of each: butcher, grave digger, doctor, music teacher, guard, baker, female elementary school teacher, midwife, miller, and shop worker. Two men were old-age pensioners, including the postman blinded in the First World War.[42]

Trevignano historians M. S. Sorrenti Terlizzi and G. Bianchi Onori relate that one of the two local shops selling food, that owned by Pietro Maracchioni on Via Umberto I (next to the alleyway leading up to the church), offered *cacio* cheese, *baccalà* (dried codfish), ham, vanilla beans, lard, coffee, liqueurs, buttons and fishhooks. Tomato sauce was sold by the spoonful. Spaghetti and maccheroni were also on offer, not packaged, but yanked from where they dangled overhead on a string.

At least some of the family names of *borgo* dwellers in the early 1700s are still common: Avincola, De Santis, Paris, Garafini, the name of the frustrated teacher of the poem. Familiar names known here since the 1800s include Catena and Neri, both with descendants who are friends today. Tancredi Gazzella was one of the shepherds; Alberto Gazzella is another good friend today. The Perconti, another familiar name today, came in the 1840s while the Palma—those of today's gas station and outstanding cinema *d'essai*—, in the 1890s. The Torregiani were early carpenters. A century or so ago Stefanelli was the first bricklayer, using not bricks but stone and mortar; the Stefanelli are still important building suppliers while other of their descendants bake the best bread in town.

Under Fascism, after 1927 the town manager was the *podestà*, with centralized powers; under Mussolini town councils were abolished. So that he could function properly, the town was obliged to supply the *podestà* with the following objects:

Writing table
Two urinals
Chest of drawers, light wood
15 chairs
Bed for 2 but not linens
2 bedside tables
2 inkwells
Brass lamp
4 glasses
2 carafes
2 kitchen knives
Tin bowl for washing dishes

The office of *podestà* was abolished only in January of 1946, when democracy came at last to Italy.

When the late Steve Jobs designed his gigantic office building in California, he had the architect make the corridors leading to the bathrooms slightly wider than normal. He also intentionally placed these bathrooms at a calculated distance from the actual office space. Why? U.S. labor economists knew that think-tank talk sessions produced only limited results, but that the famous Building 20 of MIT in Boston had outstanding results. Meticulous academic studies revealed that flexibility and casual encounters made the difference. When scientists ran into each other at the water cooler (!), this provoked a quick spurt of productive intellectual exchange—that five-minute chat in a corridor again and again. To the newest world industry Mr. Jobs, in short, adapted the functional, problem-solving stroll through the old *borgo*. And in fact, despite its loss of strategic importance after destruction of the fortress at Trevignano, today's well maintained *borgo* bursts with creativity. An example of this is its shows of *arte povero*, or poor art—little demonstrations of artworks that cost little or nothing and show the imagination at work. Among my favorites: the flower-filled wooden vegetable crates piled upon each other, atop a flight of ancient stairsteps. Another instance of creative poor art is, outside a *borgo* boutique, a dated gas pump painted a bilious green. Hard by, just for fun, are still-life "sculptures" of humble chunks of wood. Further along is a window protected by gaudily-painted pink bars. The thief the pink bars are meant to keep out would find,

Sculptor Mariano Pizzi, man of many talents.

12

Bread, Wine, Olives

Better to stink of wine
than of holy water

—Bracciano proverb

With our thirty olive trees, we harvest enough olives to make our own olive oil, which lasts us a year. In effect, thirty trees are small peanuts (admittedly, a poor metaphor); an acquaintance in Tuscany has one thousand on his estate and such a huge villa that every autumn his relatives converge from England for a family reunion and week-long revel of picking olives and partying.

Although ours is on the small scale, the production of olive oil is probably not much different than it was thousands of years ago, and until recently, only a slightly less demanding task. When we purchased our house after the death in 1993 of its first owner, my journalist colleague Dora Jane ("Dodie") Hamblin, a retired star reporter for *Time–Life* magazine, we found fifteen semi-abandoned olive trees. We went to some trouble to learn to prune those trees, as is required every second year, and then planted another fifteen. When I knew a bit more about olive trees planted on a hillside facing south, I understood that, below each tree, a half-moon should be dug to catch as much rain as possible. It was a special thrill to learn, also, that at least one in our small grove is over two hundred years old. Olive oil, not surprisingly, is among the most ancient of foods. "8,000-year-old olive oil found in Galilee, earliest known in world," trumpeted a headline in the Israeli daily *Haartez* on December 17, 2014. In the article journalist Ruth Schuster reported that, "The earliest evidence of olive oil production and use, possibly in the whole world, has been identified in pottery sherds found at Ein Zippori, in a massive Early Chalcolithic site." The date, 6000 BC, places the traces of olive oil found in this Near Eastern site to the late Neolithic, when copper tools had just begun to appear along with stone tools. No olive press has yet been found at La Marmotta, for only a small portion of the underwater site has been excavated. But among the ancient Roman farm ruins near Vicarello is, at water's edge, a millstone.

In that deep past, how was olive oil used? For seasoning foods and perhaps for cooking, but possibly also in lamps, in making soap, and in religious rituals. To keep the olives for the whole year the Etruscans who lived on our same hillside, and were buried in tombs surrounding our house, stored them in brine, as is shown in residue of amphorae found here. During the Etruscan centuries here, or after 800 BC, olives were important for eating or pressing into oil, but also apparently for sacred purposes. In the necropolis at nearby Cerveteri, olive pits were found in one of the famed Etruscan tombs, apparently left there as offerings to the dead.

When time came to harvest our olives, the families of the (now deceased) Vittorio Ruiu, a Sardinian emigre to Trevignano who had helped Dodie Hamblin over the years, and his friends Anselmo and Vittoria arrived do the picking. Under each tree they spread a net. To reach the higher boughs, they clambered up ladders. As they plucked the olives by hand, one by one, the tiny green fruits, and some which had already turned brown, dropped into the net.

Timing matters: although I have read the opposite, my experience is that the longer the fruits remain on the tree, the more oil but the less taste. The proof is in the pudding (another inappropriate metaphor): greenish oil suggests that the olives were young when picked, and hence the oil is more aromatic—though I do not doubt some oily vendors may add a hint of green coloring.

Today the picking is eased by the invention of long-handled mechanical rakes that vibrate on the branches, shaking off the olives. But the rest is the same: from the nets the olives are put into boxes to be taken to our local olive press, where they are milled on a round, flat stone into a paste, which is then put into a press. Meantime the owner

Trevignano olive orchard in springtime.

waits diligently in line to ensure that, in the end, he receives his own oil from untreated olives, rather than from someone else's (presumably) inferior olives.

Along with olive trees and oil Trevignano revels in grapes and therefore wine. The conditions are ideal: facing southward, the town looks across the lake and is flooded with sunshine. The fields are protected from the most savage winds by the ring of walls behind us which surround the caldera lake basin. For better or for worse, depending upon your point of view, the minerals of the volcanic soil which ooze into the grapes give the wine a particularly rich aroma and taste.

Did those emigres from the eastern Mediterranean, who had somehow known to paddle their way up the Arrone River to settle at La Marmotta almost 8,000 years ago, bring with them the knowledge of growing grapes and making wine? Or did the (presumably) less sophisticated locals, even if still locked into the Paleolithic, already make wine? This may have been the case. There is no hard proof of when wine was invented, but the guessing is that early people gathered berries, which they popped into that clever new invention, the baked clay pot, without which there could have been no wine, nor, for that matter, their village. Left to themselves, the berries would have rotted after a few days, leaving a sweetish liquid at the bottom of the pot. Tasting it, the pot owner liked it—and then he presumably collected more berries, this time intentionally left to ferment. What is believed the earliest known chemical evidence of wine was found in a Neolithic pot sherd, dating from 5400–5000 BC, or contemporary with La Marmotta. The wine traces were discovered in 1969 by Mary M. Voigt of the Anthropology Department of the College of William and Mary, excavating in Hajji Firuz Tepe, a settlement in the Zagros mountains in Iran. Inside a roomy mudbrick dwelling was what she identified as a Neolithic kitchen of sorts, with fireplace and storage rooms. Buried beneath its earthen floor were six 2.4-gallon jugs of wine.[43]

In one pot were both grape residue and a resin apparently used as a preservative called *terebinth*, from the *pistaci,* a tree in the cashew family. This finding is important, for it means that the wine was intentionally aged, and not merely the result of natural fermentation. Moreover, although wild grapes were available, "the wine in the jar might well have been produced from a precursor of the highly successful domesticated type (subspecies *vinifer*), still used to make modern wine," she reported.

Patrick McGovern, one of three University of Pennsylvania archaeologists also working there, is the author of *Ancient Wine: The Search for the Origins of Viniculture.* For Prof. McGovern, the history of civilization is in many ways the history of wine, which he believes was first made from wild grapes perhaps 7,000 years ago—again, more or less contemporary with La Marmotta. "As medicine, social lubricant, mind-altering substance, and highly valued commodity, wine became the focus of religious cults, pharmacopoeias, cuisines, economies and society," he writes.[44] Sometimes honey was added.

An actual winery, with a press in which grapes were stomped, was discovered in 2010 in a cave in Armenia by a team of California archaeologists. Recognized as the world's oldest yet found, it has been dated to 4100 BC, or the dawn of the Copper Age. Along with the press were found containers for fermentation and storage, ceramic drinking cups, and dried bits of grape vine, skins and seeds. "This is the earliest, most reliable evidence of wine production," said archaeologist Gregory Areshian of UCLA.[45]

The earliest wine shop in Trevignano was an *osteria* opened in 1900. In 1919, at the end of the First World War, it belonged to Enrico ("Richetto") Francesconi and his wife Lucia, mother of six. On Sunday afternoons the men from the town gathered there to play cards, eat snacks, and to talk about fishing, their animals and their farming. Wine kegs were kept at a corner of the shop in a grotto, now sealed, that had an air hole leading into a tunnel in the rock. In hot weather the grotto itself became the *osteria*, a cool place in which to nibble on tripe, tiny fried lake fish and roasted chestnuts, while sipping wine and trading anecdotes and the occasional insult, reportedly by Richetto after he had enjoyed a glass too many. The *osteria* was a part of the old wall abutting the clock tower, a stone's throw from the main palazzo that is now the town hall; facing it was a large fountain—one of two fountains in the town at that time—in which Richetto and the other vintners washed their barrels before storing their wine in the grotto close by in the hillside. This was same fountain, now long since gone, in which the village women did their washing on weekdays, and donkeys and horses drank.

Richetto's shop still exists as the Osteria La Cantinella; next door to Ermete's café (and it was Ermete, whom we shall meet shortly, who told me of its history), it has a balcony with tables overlooking the main piazza—and is warmly recommended by local Trevignanesi, not to mention Tripadvisor.

Wine is still made in Trevignano, in more or less the same way as it was in the Zagros mountains and Armenia. But here, like the jolly olive-picking event in Tuscany, in some cases the fun matters as much as the vintage. Our next-door neighbors, Ann Natanson, the widow of the Polish surrealist painter Joseph Natanson, and her adult children Phoebe and Stephen, grow their own grapes, and the harvest has been an annual autumn highlight for decades. In her touching book *Keeping the Feast: One Couple's Story of Love, Food, and Healing* (Riverhead, 2010), Paula Butterini writes of gleefully plunging into the Natanson wine barrels to stomp barefoot on the grapes. These happy moments came despite the fact that foreign correspondent Paula, covering a demonstration in Warsaw, had been severely beaten by brutal Polish police not long before her wedding to *New York Times* correspondent John Tagliabue. Worse was to come. The two had been married only twenty-three days when John was shot in the back by a sniper and nearly killed during riots in Romania. Returning to Italy, where the couple had first met, "John and I rediscovered the importance of one of the fundamental human rituals: the daily sharing of food around the family table," she wrote. For them, Trevignano was a sanctuary, and trampling the grapes, helping to make the wine at the Natansons', was a part of that sharing, and healing.

In the past, few wine sophisticates took Trevignano's commercial production seriously, but today's vintners have raised the standards. Commercial production began back in 1974, when a company called Trevignano Vino was formed. From Trebbiano, Greco, Malvasia, Sangiovese and Montepulciano grapes the fledgling company produced simple wines with simple names like Rosé del Lago and Bianco del Lago—Lake Rosé and Lake White. But with the end of the millennium the company went up-market, beginning with production of a prestigious wine, Syrah Barricato, aged eight months in oak barrels. In 2011 a second wine of quality was introduced, Sauvignon.

Novello del Lago followed, in a trickle-down process that began in Italy in the Veneto and Trentino regions, in the wake of the popularity of *Beaujolais nouveau* in France. Novello, or New, is made by putting whole grapes into steel vats, into which

Tucked into ancient wall below hilltop fortress, Osteria La Cantinella, town's earliest wine shop still exists.

carbon dioxide is pumped. The procedure, called "carbonic maceration," speeds up fermentation. The grapes are not crushed and hence the wine contains little tannin, the element from the grape skin that allows wines to age. As a result, Vino Novello, with its fairly low alcohol content of 11 percent or so, has a particularly fresh, light and fruity taste, and is consumed from autumn into the following spring.

Mirko Capitani, the co-owner of Trevignano Vino, said that his wines come from 12 hectares of land planted with vines along with olive trees on a hillside near the town. "We produce almost 50,000 bottles a year," he told me proudly, "and our production continues to rise. Our volcanic soil, the minerals, are good, and so is our exposition to the sun."

From his company's grape varieties (Trebbiano, Sangiovese, Malvasia and Montepulciano), "We expanded by reinvesting and renewing old vineyards. Ten or fifteen years ago we added Merlot and the Syrah and, more recently, white Sauvignon and Chardonnay. This year we made wine from Viognier, a white—these are new plants, ready in three years. We'd already planted Cabernet, a bit of Pinot Grigio and Franconero, a red, to blend with our Chardonnay. And Cesanese, also a red."

Every year, on the autumnal day when authorities allow Novello to go officially on the market in Italy, Capitani hosts a Novello launch, open to the public with tasting and abundant snacks. Overseeing the wine tables with him in October 2016 was Riccardo Paparella, an aeronautics officer whose hobby is being a sommelier in his spare time. Presiding over the wine tasting, Paparella was slightly more technical than Capitani about the wines of Trevignano.

"They are generally rather mineral in taste because of the volcanic soil," he explained. "These mineral salts tend to make the grapes grown here a bit strong, and some of the wines even harsh. However," he acknowledged, "this year's Novello is more *amabile* [gentle] than last year's." Indeed it was *amabile*, as was the company.

With a touch of regret I understood that Novello would not be appropriate for my Neolithic banquet: the Neolithic revolution did not include steel vats. Checking the history of the traditional grape varieties of Trevignano to find the oldest, I first considered the white wine made from Trebbiano grapes. This particularly variety originated, it is believed, from the east Mediterranean and was a favorite of the ancients. "It grows best on sun-drenched hills with hot days and cool nights," specified a wine-tasters' web site. Arriving from the east Mediterranean, popular with the ancient Romans, grown in sun-drenched hills: Trebbiano seemed made to order. But then I checked another ancient variety grown in Trevignano, Cesanese. The name was new to me, but, as I learned, Cesanese wine has a long history of production in the Roman countryside. "Quite possibly it was the red wine of ancient Rome," writes American wine sophisticate and sommelier Madeline Puckette in her blog, Wine Folly.com. Most importantly for my purposes, the variety of grape is believed to have existed here in pre-Roman times. For Puckette, moreover, Cesanese smells "like the *ichors* of wild boars, with powerful notes of cranberry sauce, sweet pomegranate, and plums."

Ichors—once the blood of the Greek gods, over time the word came to refer to the drippings from, guess what, the meat of wild boar.

Illustrating how intensely important is wine to Trevignano was the *presepe* (creche) set into the basalt wall at the end of the *borgo* one Christmas. Confected by the woman who works in the café across the street, it had a guardian angel made from

Riccardo Paparella, hobby sommelier, at Capitani launch of wines from Trevignano grapes.

an illuminated bottle. Looking more closely, I saw that the Three Kings were similarly decorated bottles, and that among the creche decorations were a tiny round café table and stool, made from wine bottle corks. And that in the crib was, get ready, a decorated cork. Above was a sign declaring *Spirito Di Vino*, words with a secular—Christmassy double meaning: Spirit of Wine and Divine Spirit.

And so to bread. That bread is a prehistoric food is beyond doubt. Known to have existed for some 30,000 years, according to archaeological evidence, it was unleavened, and in Europe was already being made in the Upper Paleolithic, well before the "civilized" Neolithic revolution. After around 10,000 BC what was essentially porridge made from ground wheat or spelt became, when baked on a stone slab, a flat bread. The Romans' flat bread was made of flour and water, shaped into a rosette, and, like the Neolithic, baked on a stone slab. Both the Etruscan and later Roman farmers of Trevignano, moreover, sold their wheat and olive oil to the other villages of the nearby countryside.

To learn about baking bread in modern Trevignano, I called upon the town's foremost baker, Alberto Pezzaglia. His bakery, like a nearby restaurant and a building supplies store down the street, is called Stefanelli, his mother's name; this is one of the town's oldest families, and all seem to be related.

In the interview at a table at the Stefanelli bakery on Trevignano's main drag, so unobtrusive that only privileged insiders notice it, Pezzaglia told me over coffee and biscuits that from the time he was twelve years old he had spent his summers working in a shop that sold baked goods. "I would help with ordering merchandise and then putting the stuff in order on the shelves." That shop, close to the main piazza, had been a little supermarket until his family bought it in 1983, turning it into what was literally the first bakery in town; until that time bread was imported from other towns. Early in the nineteenth century, he recounts, to be a baker meant, in Trevignano, to be crippled. "Being a baker meant not having to move much. He could be lame or all bent over—a fellow who couldn't do the hard work of farming or ploughing. My grandfather had this very building we are in now built, but his son, my uncle, lost an eye while he was working on its construction, and would have risked his life if he'd climbed up the scaffolding again. And that is why my grandfather opened a bakery for him, a *forno*."

For three decades, Pezzaglia's mother and two of her Stefanelli sisters owned and managed that *forno*. "I helped out the family business when I was just a child," Pezzaglia recalled, "In a garage across the street from us the women liked to make the rather expensive cookies they called *pagnotte* [loaves], which they decorated with chopped almonds and then dipped into red alchermes liqueur. This they'd top with a bit of meringue and a red cherry. When the cookie tray was full, they would bring it over to us for baking in our oven. My grandmother would count the cookies on the tray—there would be fifty—and charge 1000 lire for the baking. Then we kids would steal as many as we could get away with."

Growing up, Pezzaglia studied at a technical institute with the aim of becoming an architect, but then discovered baking, "my passion." This eventually led to his acquiring today's bakery-cum-coffee shop on Trevignano's main street, where Pezzaglia sells his stunning daily variety of breads and pizzas and sweets, as good or better than anything I ever found in Rome. His son has now opened his own bakery just off the main piazza; in it is a huge, ancient oven, newly restored.

Alberto Pezzaglia, in Trevignano's bakery, owned by his family for generations.

By tradition, Trevignano does not have its own bread. The custom is to use the traditional one-kilogram round or elongated loaf of bread with a crispy crust from Terni, called *ternano*, from Umbria, where it is generally made without salt (and hence in the past was also called *pane sciocco*, foolish bread). The reason usually given for omitting the salt is that the Pontifical State had applied a heavy tax on salt, which the bakers of Terni had refused to pay. "Bakeries in Rome still call it *pane ternano*, though they now add a lot of salt to it. We add just a little," he said.

The making of traditional bread remains a challenge, he acknowledges. "The bread has to be ready in the morning at 7 a.m., when our truck begins to make its rounds to the shops. Since it takes time for the dough to rise and for the baking, we start the evening before with flour and water, adding a bit of yesterday's dough, which is always slightly acidic, to make it rise. Then it goes into the *impastatrice,* the mixer, which can take up to 250 kilos (551 pounds) of dough." Then the bakers go home, returning to work around 3:30 a.m.

"I did this for a long time, but now, thanks to helpers, my wakeup call is later, 5:30 a.m." Even so he remains working in the store until its doors close at 8 p.m.

"People used to eat a huge amount of bread, but now that everyone is well off they eat less." Besides the traditional *pane ternano* or *sciocco*, among the other many breads Pezzaglia and his sous-chefs turn out today are a Ferrara-style bread laced with lard; fireman style or *pompiere* bread containing a hint of olive oil (the reason for the name is obscure); and varieties of rye and whole wheat breads, one of which is laced with linen seeds. One of my own favorites is called Panda bread, whose purchase goes toward a contribution to the World Wildlife Fund. Not least, and only rarely made, is what is called *pane etrusco*, Etruscan bread, made from white flour to which are added hazelnuts and raisins.

Trevignano's most authentic traditional bread is sweetened and called "the bride's pizza," *pizza della sposa*. In wealthier areas elsewhere, little boxes called *bonbonieri* made of china or ceramic filled with candied almonds (the bonbons) are offered to guests as wedding souvenirs. "Trevignano was poor, but everyone had eggs and flour, so the couple would take this sweet *pagnotta* loaf around to their neighbors and relatives as the wedding invitation. The longish loaf was topped with egg, olive oil and a bit of sugar. It would be colorful on the top, and everyone would eat it for breakfast. Today this is forgotten.

"But I remember all of this."

13

La Piazza

Close one door, and another, bigger, opens

—Bracciano proverb

One of the delights of Italian life is the piazza, and this is reflected in the language, which abounds with phrases that define the myriad roles the piazza plays. *Mettere in piazza* means put into the public domain, make it all known down to and including dirty laundry. *Scendere in piazza* is get out and do your stuff, particularly if your stuff is political. *Movimenti di piazza* are political demonstrations, *fare piazza pulita* is to clear the decks, and *contrapporre la piazza* is to go against the crowd. Other phrases I particularly like are *urlare come se fosse in piazza,* which is to shout as if you're in the piazza (this tells a lot about piazza life), and *mettersi in piazza*, strut to show who you are when others might prefer you to be more discreet.

In his recent sociological study *Piazze in Piazza*, Roman journalist Giampiero Castellotti explains that, from the time of the Greek agora and Roman forum, the piazza is the "visual memory of every town, the collective extension of individuality that represents the political dimension of life." There people "get exalted, they cringe, they succumb to pure instinct or burst into extravagant and sometimes even fatal judgements."[46]

Translated into ordinary language, the "political dimension of life" he mentions means that piazza life is about conversations and connecting, which is to say about talking: debating politics, spreading gossip, complaining, joking, squawking, shouting, insulting, moaning, flirting and occasionally praising.

In Trevignano, despite the limited space of its old walled *borgo*, several tiny *piazzette* exist in which groups can still congregate for fun, movies, lectures, music, an aperitif. With the increase in population, these *piazzette* did not suffice, and inevitably the elongated, narrow *borgo* overflowed. The possibilities for expansion were limited, however. At the eastern end of the little road slicing through the *borgo* rises a sheer wall of volcanic basalt rock; above is the steep fortress, the Rocca degli Orsini, while below is the lake. The overflow, as a result, could take place only at the western end, which is to say outside the clock tower gate to the west, where there was already the fountain shared by the village women washing clothes and the animals at a trough. In this way the big main piazza at Trevignano was created just outside the *borgo*.

Ludovico Graziani's bronze statue honors Abbot Tommaso Silvestri of Trevignano, Italy's first teacher of the hearing impaired.

In a corner just off the piazza, the village band plays.

In many an Italian city today, the lovely old piazzas have been given over to traffic roundabouts. Squeezed in between lake and mountain, this is the case in Trevignano, too, even though there was now greater space. The sole road linking Bracciano to the west and the towns and highways to the east cut straight through the piazza center, chopping it in half. The result is that there are today two piazzas which roughly form a figure eight. Between them is a big parking lot, its waistband. Despite this, Trevignano's figure-eight-piazza manages to be civilized. At the top is the larger, formal piazza, created in the 1920s from an abandoned patch of land overlooked on one side by the clock tower and, next door, the nineteenth century town hall, the *Comune*. The piazza, which is named for King Vittorio Emanuele II, has little walkways, antiquities, statues and flowered borders, where signs warn not to walk on the grass or let your dog off the leash. In the piazza are the two rough-hewn Etruscan sarcophagi. Crudely made of tuff, they evoke poverty; even the upper-crust Etruscans were simply laid to rest upon stone beds in man-made underground grottoes.

According to Trevignano journalist Franco Scalise, underlying the piazza is a rather crudely made drain pipe which a century or so ago carried the waters from the very first toilet ever built in Trevignano, running from the Palazzo del Comune all the way into the lake. Others believe that, further below, are ruins from the time of the ancient Romans, which is not unlikely.

The half of the "eight" shape adjacent to the lake is a small informal piazza known at the Porticciolo (Little Port). This traffic free, lakefront portion is in its way a vision of happiness, beloved of mothers with baby carriages, of children playing games and riding

In the piazza, bronze "Dancing Family," gift of the late Milton Hebald, American sculptor who lived in Bracciano.

In 1989, for the bicentennial celebration of Silvestri's birth, an association of Italian hearing impaired raised funds to pay for the huge bronze statue in Trevignano's piazza honoring Don Silvestri. On September 17, 1989, Pope John Paul II made a pilgrimage to Trevignano to dedicate it.

The second modern statue is "Dancing Family" by the late American sculptor Milton Hebald (1917–2015), who donated the bronze sculpture—a duplicate of that in front of the Norris Cultural Arts Center in Saint Charles, Illinois—to Trevignano. As British novelist Anthony Burgess wrote in 1971, Milton Hebald was "without doubt the most important living figure sculptor."

Hebald grew up on 97th Street and Madison Ave. Even as a child his large-scale drawings in colored chalk on sidewalks made him something of a neighborhood celebrity. When he was just eight years old a friend gave him a box of clay, which he molded. In that first instant, he later recalled, he recognized that he was a sculptor as well as an artist. As luck had it, the New York Metropolitan Museum of Art was nearby, and became his early education. He was only ten years old when he won a scholarship to the School Art League, where he enrolled in a sculpture class. The model posing for the class protested, *"I can't pose for a boy like that. Why, I've got a son at home older than he is." In high school Hebald studied at an art school by day and, in what free time remained, studied and patiently copied Old Master drawings he found in the New York Public Library. When he later saw Old Master originals in the museums, he said that it was akin to seeing an old friend.*[48]

In 1954, after winning an important commission for the Isla Verde Airport in San Juan, Puerto Rico, he and his wife Cecille Rosner came to Italy. The idea was to have the Isla Verde sculpture cast in bronze in Milan. Altogether, traveling throughout Italy and visiting its museums, they stayed nine weeks. Returning to America, Hebald applied for and won a grant to study and work at the American Academy on the Janiculum Hill in Rome in 1955. "I saw at once that what I found in Italy was what I had been looking for—the protection given by tradition, if you want to call it that," he recalled many years later. He also praised Italy's many excellent foundries, which were worked by highly skilled craftsmen.

In this way he remained in Rome for decades. For a time the couple and their daughter, Margo, lived in Trastevere, but in 1970 moved to a large wooded estate and studio he purchased on a hillside at Bracciano.

Hebald became exceptionally popular in the U.S. despite his bucking the early post-Second World War artistic trend in America, which insisted upon abstract expressionism rather than the figurative sculptures of Hebald's design. He prevailed: twenty-three of his statues are on public view in New York City alone. One particularly famous is in Central Park, and depicts Romeo and Juliet. Another of his famous works is a commissioned statue portraying a life-sized James Joyce, created for the novelist's tomb in Zurich, Switzerland.

Leaving his home and studio in Bracciano in 2004, six years after Cecille's death, Hebald died in West Hollywood, California, on January 2015 at age 97.

14

Voices

He with few coins is always counting,
He with gorgeous wife is always shouting

—Bracciano proverb

The walled *borgo* has always been so small that neighbors were and are obliged to live cheek by jowl. No one had secrets. On the contrary, the *borgo* was and is a stage, and the social interplay of its inhabitants—those walking about or seated upon the street side stone benches by day or protectively snuggled within its walls and alleys by night—is of performances. The *borgo* is the very essence of communication, speaking to us of the lives of those dwelling within, and also recounting a little of the lives of those aristocratic families who exploited its inhabitants in the past. Perhaps needless to say, the intimacy of a tiny town could also breed contempt. A quarrel in 1908 over the theft of a mattress in Trevignano resulted in a *borgo* fist fight with the allegedly guilty party getting punched and losing two teeth. That same summer three oxen damaged the vineyard belonging to *borgo* resident Giuseppe Mastrantoni, who fought back by attacking a donkey eating grain newly planted by the owner of the oxen. Similarly, a *borgo* mule driver paying scant attention to the mules in his care was punished when the mules stumbled over an object intentionally put in their way and were injured. And one Domenico Parissi snatched from its owner a horse that had damaged his fields.

"Incidents like this were all the more common because the few who owned animals had no food for them and so let them graze in fields cultivated by their neighbors," said a document from that period, found in the Trevignano archives. Not dissimilarly, and exactly like the other enclosed *borghi* that have survived elsewhere in Italy, today's Trevignano tells us of enduring customs. Communication is not only verbal, and one important communication mode is fashion. The *borgo* reminds us, for instance, why Italians dress so beautifully every day. Especially the women are decked out early in the day with makeup, hair-do's and jewelry, something that does not happen in Parisian or New York streets, where women wear sneakers on the street, while keeping a pair of "proper" shoes in a desk drawer to don when they get to work. In *borgo* or piazza, for most of the women the day begins with those proper shoes.

Cinema buff Fabio Palma (*left*) created town's first movie house in 1939. It still thrives.

Why? During the decades of poverty few had the luxury of being able to invite visitors into the mean small home in which ten lived in two rooms above their pig who kept them warm. But especially as the relative poverty gave way to a degree of well-being, the residents increased their efforts to make a fair impression upon their neighbors in the spaghetti-thin *borgo* streets and alleys that were the center of life. Thus was born that famous *bella figura,* which amounts to making a fine impression. This means that until fairly recently traditionalists could not always understand such outsiders as the wealthy American widow who had moved into Trevignano in the Sixties and always appeared in public wearing a track suit. These days this is becoming a norm, at least for some, but three decades ago the locals assumed that her lack of smart outfits meant that she was indigent. Taking pity upon her, a clique of well-intentioned local ladies took up a collection to buy her a proper frock.

In a bizarre contradiction, along with the *bella figura* came a certain amount of shouting and bumping. If you can speak to friends only in the street of a *borgo*, you must be loud to be heard, so shouting and screeching are acceptable if not unavoidable. Also, because the street is always crowded, you will inevitably bump into others and be bumped. Unless you are an outsider, no one paid, or pays, particular heed to this. I am an exception to this tolerance: being short and not exactly youthful, while walking in the *borgo* or standing at a counter waiting for coffee I tend to be bumped out of the way, usually by tall men with big bellies, of whom there is no lack. Of course this, too, is a form of communication.

Since the *borgo*, the heart of Trevignano for generations, is about various forms of communication, it is not surprising that the town developed its own dialect, compiled into a fascinating dictionary, *Come Parlavamo* (How We Spoke), by Luigia Cecchini and Aldo Lorenzini.[49] For their dictionary of 2,800 terms, published by the local Banca di Credito Cooperativo in 2006, the authors interviewed fifty Trevignano old-timers, some in their nineties. Most of the terms recorded date from the early 1900s, when the borgo was fairly crowded, and Trevignano had 1,200 inhabitants.

Where did all these local words come from? A few derived from the vulgar Roman dialect called Romanaccio or Romanesco. Others have strictly local origins. Appropriately to a town in whose back yard so many Etruscan tombs have been raided, the dialectal words include *"lo spito"* (the spike). While akin to the word in English, the spit, as in a barbecue, in Trevignano *lo spito* is site specific: it is the long prong the *tombaroli* (tomb robbers) use to probe deep into the ground to find Etruscan burial places.

In their preface, Cecchini and Lorenzini invoke a certain nostalgia for the words of the past. Today, they point out, Trevignano youngsters no longer understand some of the words their grandparents still use, for English usage has penetrated the spoken language. "Nobody says '*va bene*' [it's all right] any more—they just say 'OK'," the authors complain. "Unmarried men are not *scapole* (bachelors), but 'singles'. Hearing this, poor Grannie just sits in embarrassed silence," the authors write. Penetrating that embarrassed silence today are the high-tech words children learn from their cell phone games.

My personal favorite of the dialectal phrases is this: *'na vorta le vorpe se magnavono... mo sò tutti signori!* That is, "Once we ate foxes, but now everybody is a fine gentleman!"

Herewith a selection of the old words indicated with, first the dialect, then the word or phrase in Italian and finally my version of its English equivalent.

lo buttabanno	*Banditore*	town crier (he shouts out the *bando*, offical announcement)
Dimà	*Domani*	tomorrow
la sorràda	*Pulire sotto gli olivi*	Olive tree weeding
Fià	*partorire (specialmente animali)*	to give birth (animals especially)
Izzicà	*istigare, insistere*	instigate, insist
ce rüzzichi 'n antra vorta?	*ci risiamo un'altra volta?*	you're back at this again?
E mò m'hai stufato!	*Ormai ne ho abbastanza!*	You make me sick!
Già puzza da mortaccìno	*Già puzza di morto*	already reeks of death
Mìcco	*furbo, finto tonto, falso*	phony, sharpster
magnapà a uffa	*uno che mangia a sbaffo*	big-time glutton
macchiaròlo	*quello che va con la mandria nella macchia*	shepherd who goes to pasture with his herd
Ciò le madonne	*C'ho una rabbia*	I am cussing angry
Fostrò	*Foxtrot*	foxtrot
la fratta	*i ragazzi*	the youngsters (bro')
'ngròcca	*Gancio*	sliding knot on fish hook
'Zzoppàssi	*che ti azzoppasse*	may you go lame

On the basis of the town archives dating from 1871, the two researchers also assembled some six hundred typical Trevignano names, besides the customary Giovanni and Maria (incidentally the name of fully one-quarter of all the women in town). A goodly number of the names of both men and women ring as truly unusual, with long-lost origins. Among the women were Aldimira, Consilia, Claide, Deonizia, Laodamia, Dusia, Derna and Settilia. Men's names, also offbeat, included Cariggi, Dioscordie, Getulio, Similea, Sanquino, Verio, Folicardo and Solferino. Another typical Trevignano man's name was Sfortunato, which literally means "unlucky"; this would hardly seem encouraging, but there it is in their list of old *Trevignanesi*. And then there is Capreta, a woman's name which might almost seem to mean "little goat."

Still also frequently heard to this day are posh names, inherited from ancient history: Apollo, Diomede, Elettra, Cleopatra, Tiberio. The name Anacleto comes to Trevignano from Pope Anacletus, who died in the year AD 92; Agrippino means little Agrippa, from the Roman statesman–architect who built the original Pantheon, while the name Quintilio is inherited from the Roman general Publius Quinctilius Varus. The more exotic Zenobia harks back to the 3rd century Septimia Zenobia, queen of the Palmyrene Empire of Syria—that Palmyra with its great Roman temples recently destroyed by extremist Islamist warriors.

Then there are the nicknames, like *Baffò*, with a strong emphasis on the "o", short for *Baffone*, one sporting a hearty moustache. Another fellow to be reckoned with was known as *Satana*. Then there was *Bocca Storta*, he of the crooked mouth. *Capocciò* (short for *Capoccione*) was probably a big boss, although it would not surprise that the nickname expressed sarcasm. *Magnacaccio* would refer to a poor man, probably a shepherd, who dined on cheese (*caccio*) made from the milk of sheep (today a luxury). *Adà* was doubtless short for *Adamo*, *Sdrubbele* was a descendant variation of the Carthaginian general *Asdrubal* while *'Nezurmia* derived from *Anselma*. Not least, the woman's name *Fofa* was short for *Ippolita*, queen of the Amazons in Greek mythology.

The popular name *Toto* or *Totorello* was short for Arturo—and indeed "Totorello" was Arturo Paris, at well over ninety years of age, one of the sources consulted by the authors. He was also the subject of a documentary film made in 2012, when Toto was ninety-six, by the artist Mauro Magni, and presented at a documentary film festival by the Italian Culture Week in Havana, Cuba. *Neno* was an abbreviation of *Nazzareno*, as in the late Nazzareno Avincola, who was Truman Peeble's best friend and the founder in the Fifties of the restaurant Grotta Azzura. Nazzareno was also a cousin of the late Ermete Avincola, as in Café Ermete, the oldest and most popular café in town. But otherwise the meaning of some of the nicknames like *Gulpò, Pippitambù, Purciò, Frullina, Falocchiett,* and *Tanganè* is lost.

Today's nicknames are fairly clear. *Fridge* (in English) is the nickname of the talented amateur artist (we bought one of his paintings), who repairs refrigerators. A clever man who happens to be slender and clever too is known as *Vipero* (Viper).

Some of today's most stimulating communications in Trevignano derive from encounters in lectures and events held in the town hall and especially in the Cinema Palma, one of the town's sources of pride, across the street at the end of the *borgo*. In this vital accessory, in addition to its offerings of quality films (some in the original language), weekly lectures on art have taken place for years. The Palma is not only important in maintaining a certain cultural level in a small town, but also attracts movie

tried again and again to restart the engine, to no avail. Just then an Allied plane flew low overhead. From it a hailstorm of gunshots rained down. Palma was hit in the leg. No cars passed on the road, and hours passed before Fabio Palma was finally found, lying in the middle of the road in a pool of blood. By the time he was taken to hospital it was too late. He died at only forty-six years of age. His Balilla projector survived him. His daughter Fernanda knew where the projector had been hidden, and with her brother, Fernando, dug it out of its hole.

In 1945, the war over, the cinema was reopened. The late Fabio's longtime helper, the skillful Angelo Parissi, helped to revive the Cinema Palma, where he continued to work into his late eighties. Once again daughter Fernanda sold tickets; and when Vincenzo Marletta, the school teacher who had headed the old local Fascist party, tried to enter the movie house, Fernanda grabbed a stick and attacked him. He was only rarely seen in town after that.

This was the dawn of the era of great Italian cinema, beginning with neorealism, when the directors sought a new way of looking at reality without the propaganda of the Mussolini years. One of the very earliest was *Ossessione* by Luchino Visconti (1943). Just after the war came Rossellini's *Rome, Open City* (1946), which won the Grand Prize at the Cannes Film Festival, followed by Vittorio De Sica's *The Bicycle Thief* (1948). In the Fifties Fellini's *La Strada* was a sensation (1954), and comedian Totò won everyone's hearts. To the delight of the citizens, films from abroad like those starring the Anglo-American comedy team Laurel and Hardy were also made welcome in the Cinema Palma.

In 1954 a tornado struck Trevignano and destroyed the theater, by then a Trevignano institution. Rebuilt and expanded, such was the success of the movie house that in 1961 parish priest Don Carmelo Benedetti, concerned that movies were insufficiently

Fabio Palma (*left*), with Giorgio De Rossi, relaunched his grandfather's idea as an arts cinema.

moralizing, opened his own cinema house adjacent to the youth hospice he had already created. Asked by journalist Giustiniani whether this competition had harmed the Cinema Palma, grandson Fabio Palma responded, "No—if anything it made cinema itself more popular."

All continued well until the 1980s. By then many more Trevignanesi had the means to buy TV sets, and Cinema Palma attendance to movies dwindled to fewer than a dozen a week. By 1985 the cinema was obliged to close.

But at that point grandson Fabio Palma successfully relaunched the Palma as a quality movie house, a *cinema d'essai*. Experts said it was a folly—but it was not. Young Fabio attracted to Trevignano outstanding Italian films, which after 1994 were also presented outdoors in summertime in an arena. He also made the cinema available gratis for cultural events organized by Trevignano's town hall. And he invented the annual film festival, of which Giustiniani served as president. The Trevignano FilmFest attracted such outstanding Italian directors and actors as Pupi Avati, Gabriele Salvatores, Gianni Amelio, Francesca Archibugi and Michele Placido. It was a particular honor when Michelangelo Antonioni participated on the evening when he celebrated his ninetieth birthday in 2002. In 2018 the four-day festival included a showing of the film *Gravity*, directed by Alfonse Cuaròn. Italian astronaut Umberto Guidoni participated, telling of his personal experiences. The Cinema Palma continues today to be famous for the quality of its showings, and now has two halls plus, in summertime, its outdoor open-air theater. The latest international movie celebrity to appear before the silver screen was Glasgow-born Armando Ianucci, director of *The Death of Stalin* (2017). Lectures on the arts are still held there regularly, and films are also shown in original languages several days weekly. Grandpa Fabio would have been proud.

15

Wartime

More lambs die than sheep

—Bracciano proverb

In front of the town hall stands a white marble monument honoring the boys and men of Trevignano (no women) who died fighting in the two twentieth century world wars. On one side, guarded by the statue of a youth in doughboy uniform, are photographs of the thirty-two Trevignanesi lost during the First World War. Another thirty-two were injured, and even more suffered serious illnesses as a result of the war: Bracciano hospital records show that in 1915 alone twenty died in that hospital from the Spanish flu. Another forty-three died at home as a result of the worldwide pandemic that killed between 20 and 50 million victims.

On the back of the memorial are photos of the eleven Trevignano soldiers lost in the Second World War. Among the dead were those whose names still ring familiar today in town today—Marconi, Gazzella, De Santis, Cipollini.

In fact the wars had begun long before this. In 1909 the French-made Blériot, flown by its inventor, Louis Blériot, became the first airplane ever to fly across the English Channel. Two years later Italy declared war against the Ottoman Turks and attacked Libya. That same year, 1911, Italy began manufacturing, on license in Turin, the Blériot, which Italian pilots used for the world's first ever air bombardment. The bombs were devised by Giuseppe Cipelli at a factory at La Spezia. Each of the four carried on the plane was the size of a grapefruit and weighed over 4 lbs. To drop one, the pilot flying in the tiny open Blériot had to navigate with one hand and, with the other, lift the bomb to his mouth, and, using his teeth, carefully pluck out the pin. Then he tossed out the bomb to the target below. This, said the Italian press at the time, is "the art of winged death." Needless to say, it was less "art" than the tragedy of winged death. That war is considered a precursor to the First World War, and ended with Italy's claiming Libya as its colony; already France had laid claim to much of the North African coast (Algeria, Tunisia and, after 1912, Morocco). Rare examples of the early Blériot plane and of the Cipelli bomb itself are preserved in the Historical Museum of Military Aeronautics at Vigna Di Valle, directly across Lake Bracciano from Trevignano.

Town monument with photos of the Trevignano soldiers who died in the First World War.

After a year of lingering doubts about which side to back, in May 1915 Italy belatedly entered the war on the side of the Allied Powers. Flying the Blériot, the Italians fought against Austria–Hungary along the 400-mile border in the northern Alps. Later in the war the plane was pressed into service for five Italian squadrons. Writer Gabriele D'Annunzio (1863–1938), who was serving in the Italian air force at that time, led a flight mission of eight aircraft which dropped leaflets over Vienna in August 1918.

That June Ernest Hemingway was serving as a volunteer ambulance driver with the American Red Cross in Italy, and the following month was wounded seriously. Hemingway's novel *A Farewell to Arms* of 1929, his first best seller, tells of that experience. The female protagonist, Catherine Barkley, was supposedly inspired by the real Agnes von Kurowsky, the nurse who tended Hemingway in a hospital in Milan.

The Church could hardly ignore the war, and one hundred parishioners attended the annual assembly of the Trevignano church held October 15, 1916. Parish priest Don Antonio Bertollini, after discussion of the budget and the expenses for a funeral, made an appeal for funds for packages to be prepared by the nuns and sent to the soldiers of the IV Armata. Two declined: Giuditta Cecchini and Apollonia Ginestra, for "egotistical reasons," as the assembly minutes specified in a peevish note. As is again recorded in the minutes of that meeting, Don Antonio was less than pleased with the women of his parish, for, he declared, "If men are bad it's for the most part because of the bad examples set by women."[52]

For the duration of the First World War the church cancelled fireworks as part of the celebrations of saints' days, but reinstated them in 1920 at a cost that year of 274 lire.

The armistice ending the war on November 11, 1918, found Trevignano plunged into a severe recession. Desperately hungry farmers occupied the Vicarello baths complex with its hotel, which had been owned and managed for generations by a German monastic order. Veterans' organizations organized angry demonstrations. As a result, in 1921 the Opera Nazionale Combattenti, the national veterans' association, expropriated some of Trevignano's feudal lands and awarded plots to veterans.

The first stirrings of demands for land distribution to veterans had began on a small scale just after the First World War, when a class of farm workers who owned their own acres emerged slowly and belatedly. Complaining at the demands of the land owners, a veterans' association in Rome, backed by the government, successfully argued in 1921 for redistribution of some plots of land to those who had fought in the war, but little was changed, and the feudal reign continued. In Trevignano a group of the town's exasperated unemployed, joining the struggle demanding redistribution, first occupied the Del Drago feudal properties (pastures, woodlands, fields), then the German college at Vicarello, where they clashed with guards. It was all too little and too soon, for war returned. In 1935, only seventeen years after the end of the First World War, Italy invaded the Ethiopian Empire, also known as Abyssinia, and claimed it as a colony they named Italian East Africa. By then Italian aviation already had a fairly long history, and the Italians took there a huge number of airplanes, 390. For the first time in history the local Ethiopians, walking on foot or driving in rickety trucks on rough paths, were slaughtered *en masse* by bombs dropped from those planes.

In 1936 Italy joined an axis with Nazi Germany and in 1940 entered the Second World War on that side of the war. That June Italian forces occupied Britain's East African colonies in Eritrea, Somalia and Ethiopia. On June 2 that same year the

Trevignano youth were mobilized: once again one-third of the town population was conscripted.

Local accounts have it that, until their retreat began, most of the German troops still in the area behaved, by and large, in a friendly way. Because Trevignano was relatively unimportant, and there was no nearby partisan activity, the German troops appeared relaxed and relieved from the stress of war by enjoying time on the beach (!) According to architect Franco Mezzetti, writing in *Trevignano Romano* in 1969, "The Trevignano population adapted to the new regime, closing itself into a calm and detached serenity, all given over to work in the fields and the shops. No episodes of violence on the part of the Black Shirts took place in Trevignano, just as there were no active manifestations of anti-Fascism on the part of the citizens."[53] Perhaps. But nevertheless, as Maciucchi records, "weapons of war were secreted in the olive orchards." Including ours? Perhaps.

The SS command was headquartered in a building in Bracciano. In Trevignano itself Nazi officers settled into a gracious 1920s villa overlooking the lake; in front of it was a small stone cottage the Nazis used to store munitions, as a man who had been a child at the time told me. The munitions were brought in by plane and then boat, and from Trevignano, forwarded to Germans occupying inland towns, he recounted.

During the war Nazi troops also occupied Vicarello, the gigantic estate with hot springs that had once belonged to Roman emperors. In the 1930s, on orders from the west German Rhineland, the male monks of the German–Hungarian College had turned the estate over to the German nuns of Our Lady of Mulhausen. The nineteenth-century hospice there was converted into a hospital for wounded German soldiers, who were tended by these German nuns. Two of the Vicarello nuns were Italians, Sister Maria Sebalda and Sister Maria Lucrezia, dispatched to Trevignano as teachers in the little school donated by the man still known as the prince of Trevignano, Tuscan-born Piero Ginori Conti (1865–1939). When a German patrol captured five men from Trevignano who had been hiding out, they ordered them to be shot. Learning of the five arrested Trevignanesi, Sister Sebalda, who was already especially popular among the *Trevignanesi*, intervened to negotiate their release. The five were spared.

Food rationing was less severe than in the big cities, we are told, but the tensions of war took its toll on civilians nevertheless. To escape the air raids, the townspeople would rush to hide in gutted Etruscan tombs in the hillsides above town and in ancient grottos high on La Rocca. A 1940s photo of Trevignano schoolchildren with their teacher shows the stress: the children, thin and unsmiling, sit with arms crossed across chest as if for protection.

In an extraordinary turnabout in alliances, in early July of 1943 British and American troops successfully attacked Sicily and, from there, began the northward thrust toward Rome. On July 24, 1943, with the backing of that King Victor Emmanuel who had previously supported Mussolini, the Grand Council of Fascism ousted the Duce. Overnight, in central and southern Italy, those who had been Mussolini's German allies became the enemy, and the Anglo–Americans, the former enemy, the ally. The country was split in two. The old Italian seaplane base at Vigna di Valle attracted fighter planes from England and the U.S. Lake Bracciano, which was on an air route between Rome and the north, became the setting for savage war operations. "The sky became a transit stage for gigantic foreign military planes and, often, into a space for dueling aviators," town historian Maciucchi recorded. In one such duel, which took place on July 8, 1943, an American pilot, Flt Lt. W. A. Rabone, strafed and destroyed three Italian

During Second World War bombings, residents hid in Etruscan grottos on hillside below fortress.

Z506B airplanes called "Flying boats" that were at anchor in the hydroport at Vigna di Valle (that already venerable seaplane base which would later become Italy's national aeronautics museum). The duels terrified the inhabitants, who took refuge once more in the grottoes on the Rocca Romana hillside.

A Texas regiment, heavily armed, advanced from Rome along the ancient Via Cassia and then approached Lake Bracciano at Anguillara. Since the road between Anguillara and Trevignano had been destroyed, the Texans proceeded on the south side of the lake, past Vigna di Valle toward Bracciano. Their entire advance of fifty-five miles, from Rome to the Tyrrhenian coast and Piombino, lasted twenty-nine days. By July 1, the Allies had taken five thousand enemy prisoners. A vivid account of their advance is recorded in the Texas Military Forces Museum at Austin, Texas:

> The enemy [German troops] was completely confused. His battered divisions were scurrying north to avoid annihilation while fresh units were brought in to try to stave off the inevitable. A company of bicyclists, some 200 men recently hurried in [by the Germans] from Denmark, were thrown into the line in time to combat the full weight of the 36th's assault battalion near Lake Bracciano. This unique organization was crushed before it tasted battle. For the enemy, the move had been futile—practically all the troops were captured, along with their bicycles. Nothing remained to hamper the progress of the 36th as it rolled twenty-five miles into the port of Civitavecchia.
>
> Through the Lake Bracciano–Manziana sector, the Division plodded on, coping with sporadic resistance as Germans vainly attempted to delay our troops. Swinging west toward the coast, the "Texas" Division mopped up German remnants in its path to Civitavecchia, important Italian port which had fallen the same day to the 34th Division. Continuing north to Tarquinia, the 361st Infantry, attached to the 36th, met and overcame bitter German opposition.[43]

Rome, Bracciano, Civitavecchia: this was the same route taken by ancient Roman soldiers as well as by their later barbarian enemies. Before their final retreat to the north in June of 1944, German bombers had incidentally destroyed stretches of Trajan's Aqueduct which had survived barbarian invasions.

As for Mussolini, following the surrender of the Italian government to the Allies, King Victor Emmanuel had informed the Duce on July 25, 1943, that, "The game is over. You will have to go." But this generated a new problem: in what amounted to a movable house arrest, the new government headed by Marshal Pietro Badoglio, fearing that the Germans would seize Mussolini, kept him moving from place to place in secret for the next two months. At that point Hitler convoked Otto Skorzeny, head of an SS Panzer Brigade, and personally ordered him to find and rescue the Duce. In mid-August of 1943, six weeks after the Allied victory, an informer whispered to Skorzeny that Mussolini had been moved to a villa on the Isle of the Maddalena, off Sardinia. To continue to hide him, two weeks later, on August 28, the new Italian government, allied with the Americans, had Mussolini moved to, of all places, Bracciano. His stay on the lake did not last long. Sent on to the isle of Ponza, just off the Tyrrhenian coast south of Rome, Mussolini was again transferred on September 1 to the Hotel Campo Imperatore, a ski resort high on the Gran Sasso in the Abruzzi mountains. By then the Germans had located him, and in a dramatic air operation seized Mussolini.

During all that time soldiers from Trevignano had endured the war and often prison, some in Germany, some in the U.S. Some were imprisoned in both those countries, as Pasquale Tridente tells us.[54] Tridente, born in 1957, began his career as a Carabiniere and ended with silver and gold crosses for valor. As a military officer he toiled in rescue operations after the 1980 Irpinia earthquake in southern Italy, in which 2,483 died and 7,700 were injured. In 2008 Tridente began collecting the reminiscences of the aging Trevignano veterans of the Second World War. Among these veterans was Alvio Cecchini, born in Trevignano in 1921. Sent to Russia when he was just twenty years old, Cecchini was in a division of two hundred eighty. Of these only seventy—one out of four—survived. As he related to Tridente, when their buses failed to appear he and his comrades had walked almost five hundred miles from Budapest to Bucharest and on to Moldavia. From there their march continued on to Dnepr in the Ukraine and then Kiev and Bielorussia. At Bonskiro on the River Don they fought against troops he defined as "Mongolian" before coming under attack by Russian troops. After that battle, in which many Italian soldiers were lost, "We had plenty of horsemeat to eat." That is, the soldiers who had been accompanying the horses had been killed.

Tridente also interviewed Arturo Paris, born in 1915. Paris recounted that he had been sent to the Greco–Albanian front in 1942, but he and his fellow soldiers found themselves completely without food and famished. "So as to eat, we boiled shoes that were made of cowhide. They had to be cooked for a long time." One day in 1944 Paris was captured and deported to a German prison camp. With other prisoners he was taken to work in the fields. Coming across a field of daisies, the prisoners were so hungry that they leapt upon them and ate them. "Within a few days we had emptied that entire huge field."

Another soldier was Arideo Paris, born in 1913. His regiment of the Treviso Artillery participated in the unopposed Italian occupation of Albania, but later he was sent to the Greek–Albanian front. There they were given such poor quality weapons that one imprecise old canon, when fired, shot off in all directions, "killing some of our own infantry." Learning that Arturo Paris, a relative who was also from Trevignano, was nearby, Arideo managed to slip away from his post to join Arturo. Because it was late in the evening, he remained with Arturo's platoon and slept there. On returning the next morning he found that his own refuge had been blown to bits. His visit to Arturo had saved his life.

Arideo Paris was in Yugoslavia in 1940 when he and thirteen fellow Italian soldiers were attacked by Communist partisan fighters. After a brief battle all fourteen were taken prisoner. "We thought we would be shot, but then I had an idea. I took off my belt and dropped my trousers to show I had to pee. They let me, and I moved into a crevice in the rocks," he told Tridente.

> Since this left me out of sight of the partisans, I stayed hiding in the rocks. With me I had some hand grenades which I hid there so that, if I were captured again, they would not get them. I hid there a long time, and heard shots and machine gun fire. A fellow soldier named Zingaretti also managed to escape, and told me that the partisans had killed all the others. Then our reinforcements arrived, and there was a brutal battle that left many dead.

Sent with his regiment to Lubiana, Slovenia, in 1943, Arideo Paris was taken prisoner once more. This time the German soldiers had him deported to Germany, where he was put to work first on a farm and then in a factory. The German guards considered him too slow a worker, and insulted and struck him.

> We slept in wooden barracks that were so cold at night that, to make a little fire, by day we would grab a few chunks of coal and hide them in our underpants.
>
> But I got caught one evening, when a guard had a German shepherd jump me. The dog bit me on the head. Then I was arrested and put into isolation in a prison in a wooden barracks. Once the door closed you could only stand up. Near the door was a guard who never left me out of his sight. I feared I would be shot and never see my loved ones again. But after twenty-three days detention I was put on trial and acquitted. An interpreter said I could go back to work. My prison ended only in June of 1945.

At about the same time Paris was captured in Slovenia, the Allies advancing north from Rome had bombed the Via Cassia, which became littered with "animal remains, cannons, trucks, mini-trucks, and people walking sorrowfully," as the future architect Angelo Cecchini, still a child at that time, related. For some this was manna from heaven: a Trevignano mechanic known as "Sor Vittorio" would sneak out to collect the metal car parts, which he would then restore and reassemble into motorcycles, which he rode into Rome to sell, returning at night by bus.

Until recently divers in the waters of Lake Bracciano would occasionally come upon propellers and, not infrequently, bullets and hand grenades. In September 2017, when the lake water had receded due to drought, poor aqueduct maintenance and exploitation by the privatized water company in Rome, panicky early morning swimmers spotted on the public beach at Trevignano a Second World War German hand grenade known as a "potato masher." Carabinieri and army officials immediately cordoned off the beach until the grenade was removed. This was nothing particularly new. Already during the previous year some forty Second World War bombs and bits of artillery had been found in the waters between Trevignano and Anguillara. And that very September sixteen more bombs and grenades were found.

Today the war memories are distant enough that in November of 2017 the traditional Trevignano trattoria Grotta Azzurra organized a dinner honoring wartime cuisine, to help publicize a new cookbook published by Fefè Editori (Fefè is an old Trevignano name, incidentally). The book written by Leonardo de Sanctis was based upon his finding a dusty manuscript kept by his mother and marked simply "Ricette di Guerra." These war recipes were originally written by his great-aunt Amalia de Sanctis. The Grotta Azzurra dinner menu was based upon the recipes:

Crostini con stracchino e acciughe	Toast tidbits with cream cheese and anchovies
Pasta e ceci al rosmarino	Rosemary-flavored pasta and chickpeas
Involtini di cavalo con crocchette di patate	Stuffed cabbage rolls served with potato croquettes
Torta di ricotta e mandorle e torta di riso	Rice and ricotta cheesecake with almonds

Buon apetito!

16

Peacetime

Let me be farm boss for one year,
If I don't get rich, it's out of here

—Bracciano proverb

At the end of the Second World War Italy lay in tatters, its politics, economy and society trashed by the two decades of Fascism and by a war that had seen the country's government overturned and its Nazi occupiers ousted by the Allies. Over 300,000 military died in that war, as did at least 153,000 civilians. Millions more were injured, and 90 percent of the country's infrastructure was destroyed.

Near Trevignano the Via Cassia had been bombed by the Allies, and on it lay "animal remains, cannons, trucks, mini-trucks and people walking sorrowfully," in the words of architect Angelo Cecchini, relating his childhood memories of Trevignano. Because the road between Trevignano and Anguillara was also destroyed, crops were taken to the Anguillara market by rowboat. At that time two out of three in the Trevignano territory were farm workers, and an estimated eight out of ten were illiterate. Few in Trevignano had electricity, and for many in the *borgo* the only light in the home by night was the scant public outdoor lighting that passed through a front window. Still, the end of the war brought happiness: the end of Fascist rule, the birth of democracy and, slowly, economic revival. For Trevignano specifically, the aftermath of war also marked the end of the lingering traits of that feudalism which had resisted for over seven centuries. These traits did not die overnight: at the end of the Second World War the town and its lands were still called a *"feudo,"* or feudal landholding. This tradition most extraordinarily dated from at least the early thirteenth century, when the territory belonged to the Curtabraca and then the Di Vico families, feudal lords who owned the pastures, fields, woodlands and, often, the lake itself at Trevignano.

Feudalism ended only slowly. In 1896, Piero Ginori Conti, grandson of Cosimo Conti, became the feudal owner of Trevignano. Just three years later the Court of Cassation, Italy's supreme court, officially proclaimed Piero the "Prince of Trevignano." Born in Florence in 1865, Piero was graduated with a degree in social sciences from the University of Florence and later awarded honorary degrees from the Universities of Pisa and, perhaps surprisingly, Pennsylvania. By all accounts Piero was gifted, if not without flaws; one of these was his support for Mussolini. Rather than the princedom of Trevignano, his primary interests were business and science. In 1904, when he was almost forty, he took charge of an already important company founded by his wife's great-grandfather at Lardarello, near Volterra. The company produced boric acid, which was readily found in Tuscany and widely used in agriculture. Under Piero, the Lardarello company became ever more successful, especially after he devised a method for converting geothermal power, or natural dry steam geysers, into electricity. In 1912 he had the first geothermal power plant installed at the village of Larderello. Within four years it was distributing 2,750 KW of electricity in the surrounding area.

In 1896 Prince Piero was elected to the Italian Parliament to represent Volterra. He eventually served three legislatures while also promoting apparently philanthropic causes, such as sports clubs for youth. His clubs, however, seem to have evolved into Fascist dens, and Piero reportedly organized Fascist *squadristi* punishment expeditions in the countryside around Volterra.

By 1939, with Italy on the verge of the Second World War, Prince Piero's Larderello plants were generating electricity for Mussolini's steam-driven railway trains. Most conveniently, the government purchased those plants. That same year Mussolini brought Piero to Rome and into the government as a cabinet minister. During the depression years leading up to the Second World War a number of the once productive farms and vineyards of Trevignano had been abandoned. As war approached its prince had little time to spend in Trevignano. And then, on September 1, 1939, Nazi Germany invaded Poland, which marked the beginning of the Second World War. Minister Piero Ginori Conti died just three months later, on December 3, 1939.

For Trevignano, the situation worsened in the dramatic wartime months of 1943, when the town was on the front line. "At the end of World War II the soldiers returning home found the same sorry spectacle that their fathers had at the end of World War One. Poverty had returned where there had been well-being," wrote historian Maciucchi.[55]

Not surprisingly, civil strife grew. Throughout Italy agitation for land redistribution burst onto the political agenda during the late 1940s and in Calabria and elsewhere some of the early postwar protests turned violent. This did not occur in Trevignano, where lake fish were sufficiently abundant that, despite still having to turn over a portion of the catch to the feudal owners, the fishermen were fairly prosperous. Nevertheless the fishermen took the radical step of forming a cooperative, which amounted to an attack on the medieval status quo.

The problems were more difficult for the farmers. At the end of the Second World War the sole road linking Trevignano with the outside world was the one leading to Bracciano, but this had been ravaged by a few errant bombs and by giant German trucks. The road to the other lake town, Anguillara, was already lost, and so transport of crops from Trevignano could be solely by boat. The neediest townspeople survived on a bread ration. As one of the town street sweepers confided to me in 2017, "Seventy years ago the mattress of my father's bed was made of corn husks. Under his bed slept a pig, and above it, chickens on a rack." As I subsequently learned, one reason for keeping a pig under the bed was that it kept the sleeper above on a corn husk mattress warm.

On June 2, 1946, the country held a referendum on their future form of government. Eighty-nine percent of the citizens turned out to vote, including for the first time women, and elected a republic to replace the monarchy, 54.3 percent against 45.7 percent. This

17

Strolling

Monks, priests and chickens
are never ever found alone

—Bracciano proverb

Today, as cities like Rome grow ever larger, more polluted and more crowded, and cars and electric bicycles and *motorini* (scooters) jam the roads, *la passeggiata* has become something of an endangered urban species. This makes it all the more pleasurable that the stroll survives here and there, and never better than in our small town a convenient hour's distance from Rome. With *la passeggiata*, Trevignanesi need never be alone. To stroll is to be a participant. One description of it comes from a certain distinguished British scientist, who once told me that, as a young man from windswept Yorkshire, he was visiting Sicilian friends who lived on the fashionable Viale della Libertà in Palermo. On his first Sunday morning there, he was awakened by an unusual torrent of noise. He rushed to the window, threw open the shutters, and saw, for the first time in his life, *la passeggiata*. "The ladies in flowery silk frocks walked arm in arm with their husbands, dressed in full suit, white shirt and tie. I'd never seen anything so wonderful!" His face turned sad. "Too bad our climate doesn't allow anything similar."

He did not yet know that *la passeggiata* in Palermo was also known as *lo sdruscio,* the slide-by, because the young heifer lads out strolling à la Fellini film would try to graze, with knee or elbow, one of the the girls walking arm-in-arm with her sister or best friend.

Trevignano's *passeggiata* begins at the piazza by the port—the *porticciolo*—which connects on either side to a broad walkway that extends for well over a mile. This long walkway, designed by architect Franco Mezzetti back in the Sixties, is beloved of strollers, joggers and dogwalkers all day long, but especially on weekends and holidays; alongside it are literally scores of cafés, restaurants and fairly intimate beach areas with chaises longues for hire. The walkway can be crowded, but is sedate unless one considers the dogs growling at each other.

The stroll is usually celebrated as a metaphor, as in "a stroll through history," but the stroll on its own does not seem to have been considered a worthy subject. However, as a veteran of decades of strolling hither and yon, I know that the Italian way of strolling is

For Trevignano strollers, a 1½ mile shoreline *passeggiata*, with Sunday market.

more than a function of a balmy climate. Its important social consequences were honed in the ancient walled *borghi,* like that at the heart of Trevignano beneath its crumbled castle.

Where scattered small towns existed for centuries under the threat of marauding armies from the north of Europe, the *borghi* were given walls. Locked at night to keep out the enemy, their stout gates were opened only in the mornings to allow the country folk to walk out to till their fields and tend their flocks. The locked *borgo* was the sole safety measure, whose importance was further accentuated by its keeping the women confined within the *borgo* unless it was time to do the washing in the lake.

In times of prosperity, the *borgo* population surged, and each household would expand to have seven or eight children. The cramped household was chaotic, and visitors were rarely invited to drop into a two- or four-room house in which ten people lived. This continued into the Sixties if not longer. What existed instead was the *passeggiata*, and little more than that. The outdoor stroll within the walls permitted a family show of power. It allowed an old person to be taken out for a walk leaning on the arm of a son or daughter. It put on display a young girl hoping for and indeed requiring marriage. On the *borgo* street benches were added so that the elderly and the females could sit outdoors and gossip.

Raniero Monaco Di Lapio's Elvis, while still a baby pet pig.

establishments throughout Italy, from the Campania through Tuscany, Emilia-Romagna and Lazio including, needless to say, Trevignano Romano.

Dogs are not the only pets seen on leashes along the *passeggiata*. The successful and handsome actor and Trevignano resident Raniero Monaco Di Lapio has had a tiny pet piglet named Elvis. When he would take Elvis for a lakefront stroll, the piglet upstaged every last dog on the walkway. At least he did: over time Elvis has grown into a full-sized but still loving and lovable Big Pig—albeit too big to be brought to the beach any more.

18

Café Society

Chit-chat is only half a loaf

—Bracciano proverb

Over time I have tried to imagine those who lived in Trevignano long ago: the men during the Paleolithic era stretching to reach the fruit on the trees to feed wandering little bands, the women in the huts of the Neolithic village giving birth and tending to their tiny children. The Etruscan villagers molding pots of black clay to emulate bronze, which they could not afford; the Roman aristocrats lounging and gossiping in the hot baths at Vicarello; the medieval workers bent under the weight of the blocks of tuff they carried uphill to build the castle atop the Rocca Romana; the early sixteenth century craftsmen painting the frescoes in the Church of Santa Maria Assunta after studying the sketches made by Raphael or Paolo Romano. But then today's reality must also enter the picture. Bracciano and Anguillara Sabazia are partly dormitory suburbs because connected by fairly fast trains to Rome, and this inflates their size; each has around 19,500 residents. The relatively isolated Trevignano Romano remains miniscule by comparison: with exactly 5,700 residents representing 3,000 families in 2018, it is the sole lake settlement to remain a village. Many living here are retirees; in Trevignano in 2019 one out of four, or 25 percent, was over 65—that is, 2 percent higher than the national average, according to the central statistics agency ISTAT. Admittedly, they seem more, and no matter what the weather, its cafés are busy all day long, and are jolly well into early evening. Everywhere and at any hour until evening it is almost always time for a coffee break, which gradually eases its way into the *aperitivo* hour, celebrated with a glass of prosecco. This is in stark contrast with the sad coffee scene in Edward Hopper's 1942 oil-on-canvas painting *Nighthawks*. You know it well: two men and a woman sip coffee at the counter of an all-night, big-city diner-café, grimly illuminated by the new-fangled fluorescent lights. Both the men wear hats, like the one my father always wore.

Here in summer some men wear straw hats and a few, baseball caps as they enter the main piazza in Trevignano, home to no less than five cafés. Only steps away are more, each with its special charm, each with its clientele of habituees, each with a few chairs and tables outdoors. Even the gas station on the outskirts of town has a friendly café with tables and, outside, a covered area where drivers waiting for a car to be washed or a tire changed can sit and recover from road rage. Or (more likely) just sit, chat and enjoy life. On a Sunday morning church-goers congregate in the cafés, jostling for place at the counter with cyclists in their ultra-bright, ultra-tight britches and T-shirts, who themselves must weave their way through the people with dogs at their feet, including me.

In Rome, some cafés sparkle with the shiny marble that is the café equivalent of bling. In certain cases this can intimate dodgy ownership, as in recycled funny money. For instance, Doney's on the famous Via Veneto was a personal favorite of mine, but recent court reports have detailed meetings there of Sicilian mobsters as well as tourists. Another favorite just across the street, the Café de Paris, was shut down in 2014 after a suspicious fire, which occurred shortly after its links with the Calabrian 'Ndrangheta were revealed.

Both these bling cafés were most associated with Fellini's *La Dolce Vita* in the Sixties. But there were other interesting cafés, some in unexpected places. During my six years of work at the U.S. Embassy, just off Via Veneto in Rome, I would sometimes forsake the Dolce Vita cafés to steal into the bleakly serious, in-house coffee bar of the Communist-dominated General Confederation of Italian Labor (CGIL), where my inexpensive Marxist cappuccino was antidote to a certain narrowness of

Lively summer evening at Café Ermete (right of clock tower).

embassy perspective. I have also found hospitable cafés inside hospital lobbies, where patients toss a raincoat or bathrobe over their gowns and pyjamas and lean against the counter while chatting with anyone who will listen about their operation or new baby.

For most of us, what is consumed in a café in the morning begins with the cappuccino. Calculating a minimum of 320 daily presences in Italy per year, with one cappuccino at 8 o'clock in the morning and another at 11, in the past six years or so I have sipped, and only very rarely spat out, 2,560 cappuccini. To make a proper cappuccino is a delicate business. The foam cap must have precisely the right, creamy consistency, for it keeps the cappuccino warm. A foam overdose—where you can actually see bubbles—will cool down the cappuccino. To avoid this, the barman or woman at any self-respecting café lets the steamed milk rest a moment, then bangs the metal pan on the counter to remove the unwanted big bubbles (today's filip is for the barman to twist the foam into a heart).

Along with the cappuccino I begin the day with a cornetto (the Italian version of the French croissant) as well—one never, ever made from mass-produced frozen dough and preferably made in the café itself. The name refers to the two little horns poking up at each end, and it is baked from a twisted dough, preferably made with butter rather than margarine or lard. The shape is always the same, but once baked a cornetto comes with variations: plain with sugar glazing; without sugar (salty, or *salato,* my favorite at Ermete's); or given an abundant filling of jam, creamy pudding or, yuk, chocolate. The health-minded will prefer one baked from whole wheat flour with a smear of honey.

Many like to dip their cornetto into the cappuccino. In his 1964 candid camera show "Specchio segreto" (*Secret Mirror*), actor Nanni Loy made Italy roar with laughter by dipping his cornetto into the cappuccino of a startled workman in Bologna. Here what was truly amusing was the fact that almost all of the men standing at the bar, into whose coffee cups Loy intrusively dipped his cornetto, simply laughed and offered to buy him his own cappuccino.

As everyone knows, even in cosmopolitan Trevignano to order a cappuccino at the end of a meal, or, heaven forbid, in the middle of the afternoon, is *un'americanata*, pronounced with a sneeringly nasal *"ata"* at the end. This refers to a style or action so vulgar that only us Americans will do it. Never mind that the word is often spoken derisively by an Italian decked out in tight blue jeans, T-shirt with a slogan in English, baseball cap with LA on it, and gaudy sneakers made in China.

Especially in the morning fray, the café can become a scene of wild movement. As the crush of customers heaves and shoves and elbows toward the front of the bar, jockeying for space and attention, the barman or, as of recently, barwoman, must somehow remember the orders and then, out of the chaos, create order by matching the fare to be served with the face he or she may be seeing for the first time.

He or she must also remember its myriad variations. The cappuccino, for instance, is rich with milk, but can be served the old-fashioned way, in a glass (*nel bicchiere* or *in vetro*), or in a thick pottery cup (*in tazza*). From there the consumer proceeds to specify how much or little foam is desirable (*poco schiuma*, *senza schiuma*). As for the simple *espresso*, this too comes in countless variations:

"Un caffè."	(Don't fool with it. Add nothing. This is serious.)
"Un caffè macchiato."	(Dash of milk. I'm the fancy type. Preferably heated.)
"Un latte macchiato."	(Dash of coffee added to hot milk.)
"Un caffè corretto."	("Corrected" with a dollop of brandy. Favored by street people and serious blue-collar workers.)
"Un ristretto."	(Especially concentrated, for tough guys with strong appetites.)
"All'americano."	(Thinned down with water into a timid broth.)
"Doppio."	(Double dose, for those in dire morning distress.)
"Freddo."	(Cold.)
"Scecherato."	(Shakered," or tossed in a blender with ice.) And so on.

In Rome, over the noise, the barman in his black cummerbund shouts the order down the counter to his colleague manning the coffee machine, then slams a saucer in front of each customer—larger if for cappuccino, smaller if for caffè—and places a spoon onto the saucer in a specific position: one o'clock, three o'clock, six o'clock. Like the knots in strings made by the Incas, each spoon position tells a story, as I learned when I once absently shifted my spoon and found myself being shouted at.

Other conventions must also be respected. When a customer in one Trevignano coffee bar—not Ermete's—requested a glob of whipped cream for his cappuccino on a sweltering August morning, the pretty girl serving objected. In a glass bowl whipped cream was there and visible, a luscious Mount Everest. But she pointed out that this was high summer, and that the whipped cream was for ice cream cones only. Anyway, the morning was too hot to think about adding whipped cream to a cappuccino, she said. Instead of stammering a lame apology, the customer objected stubbornly that in his cappuccino he liked whipped cream all year round, every day.

From the little knot of habitués who overheard the exchange came snickers. They knew what the waitress's response would be. They watched as, performing for her audience, she scornfully filled the cappuccino to the brim and topped it with a giant dollop of whipped cream—filled it until it spilled over, making a brown puddle in the saucer of the poor customer, who had no choice but to drink it all up while ignoring the guffaws, even as dribbles from the cup slopped down the front of his nicely ironed shirt with its fancy label. I sympathized, for as a *connoisseur* I too have special requirements, which are in fact demands. No matter how hot the temperature outdoors or in, I order my cappuccino *bollente* (boiling), although many Italians prefer theirs tepid. For the barman to steam the milk until it is hot takes extra time. He or she gives in, but sometimes with a grumbled, "Me, I couldn't drink it that hot." Once in a café in Rome a die-hard waiter fixed me with a spiteful stare that said, "I'll fix her," and then made it as fiery hot as he could—a foretaste of hell. These are the same barmen, needless to say, who ignore their customers while courteously trotting out from behind the counter to feed a customer's dog a tasty morsel from one of the sandwiches behind the glass counter.

Speaking of pets, one morning over coffee at Ermete our friend Mario made a stunning confession. He lived on a farm just outside town, where he had two dogs. In addition, he said, he had a pet boar. "A wild boar?" I exclaimed. "Well, not wild. Here's what happened." One morning he saw a tiny animal in the road. Thinking it was a kitten, he stopped the car and got out to rescue it. But it was not a kitten. It turned out to be a baby boar.

"Still, I felt sorry for it. It was injured. I couldn't stop myself from picking it up and taking it home. Taking *her* home." He fed it with a baby bottle and foods he cooked especially—pasta was a favorite—, until the boar was cured, and growing. Still he kept her. "I'd planned on releasing her into the wild, but eventually realized I'd put her on a human schedule: awake by day, asleep by night. Boars do just the opposite. And I knew that in the end if I released her, a hunter would shoot her."

Six years later Emma (as he calls her) still lives with Mario. Not only: she comes up to kiss him, she lies beside him on the grass and, when he plays dead, she carefully raises his legs and arms.

A special challenge in another of my favorite cafés in Trevignano, La Vela, is to get a look, for free, at the morning newspaper. Thrown atop one of the tables, it would already be stained, with the sports pages curled up and scarred brown from others' beverages. In Trevignano, as in Rome, the newspaper on the table is a statement of the politics of the owner. At La Vela that paper was usually *Il Tempo*, which has a rightist tinge, although it can be interesting. To get at it required ingenuity in the daily battle with the other regulars, who wanted to pour endlessly over the soccer reports and the articles denouncing immigrants. Few *tifosi* (fans) were about to be put off by a woman, uninterested in sports, and a foreigner to boot.

The trick, then, was to walk inside, and immediately check to see if the paper was free, then pin it down, setting up a beachhead while simultaneously ordering. One must begin reading before someone else arrives to grab the paper. If the morning enemy succeeds, there it goes, and for ten minutes I'd hear nothing but disgust at what *la Juve* did to *la Roma* or *il Lazio*.

Still, three days out of four, I managed to get to the newspaper first—though not without a fight. And perhaps that was part of the fun.

In Trevignano café society two individuals stand out as the town's quintessential citizens. The late Ermete Avincola was an insider from an old Trevignano family. When I interviewed him two years before his death in 2018 he was still handsome, still interesting, and still seen most mornings inside the café that bears his name. It was the town's first cafe and is still its most popular, where the cappuccini are close to perfection, as are the pastries including the *cornetti*.

The other quintessential Trevignanese is Truman Peebles, who is at this writing one hundred and eight years old. An American born in New Jersey, he vaunts a PhD in psychology and has lived in Trevignano for over sixty years. On many a morning he can still be seen seated at a table at one of the cafés, outdoors on a sunny day or inside if the day is chilly.

My interview with Ermete took place in February of 2016. We spoke in front of a fire glowing in the fireplace in the roomy apartment where he lives above the café that bears his name. Downstairs, behind the café is its bakery and in the basement below, a wine bar. In front of the café is its glassed-in veranda and, beyond that, a big apron of tables on the *sampietrini*, where people sit outdoors under umbrellas when it is sunny. Many also sit outdoors even in winter, unprotected, no matter how inclement the weather.

Born in Trevignano, the late Ermete Avincola (here at age 85) owned Café Ermete for decades.

Ermete's café snuggles inside a line of buildings, topped by the eighteenth-century clock tower that straddles the original gate into the old *borgo*. This stretch of buildings is its own story. By more or less modern times the V-shaped medieval walls that ran down from the hilltop castle to the round fort at lakefront had been removed to recycle the stones, which is a polite way of saying they were stolen. The connecting wall down which sentries and soldiers once walked is therefore mostly gone. However, just above and below the *borgo*, a surviving stretch of the old thick wall has remained, and in centuries past the custom was to dig little caves into these vestiges to house people, animals and little shops.

Today, as I have written in Chapter 10, "Fortress," despite the plaster-covered sections, a hefty portion of that defensive wall still exists, stretching all the way down to the old round watch tower at lakefront, where it backs up against the elegant summer tables of a modern restaurant.

In the early nineteenth century a tiny general shop that sold everything from matches to spaghetti was located adjacent to the gate that opens into the *borgo*. When it went out of business in 1930, Costantino Avincola, Ermete's father, purchased the little shop, which became the café that has ever since been a focal point of Trevignano's social life. It has even acquired a bit of international renown: one day in March 2017 Ermete's Café was shut so that a scene from a movie starring Cuban–American actor Andy Garcia could be filmed there.

Costantino Avincola's wife was Maria ("Marietta") Baiocca, a "*mammana*," or trained obstetrician born in the Marches. Employed by the state, she had come to Trevignano, having won a place after a competition, and there she met her husband, Costantino.

"For decades my mother gave birth to every infant born in Trevignano," her son, the Ermete whose name still graces the café, told me during our interview the summer before he died. "Until 1950 we were the only café, and between births, she ran it," he added with pride. "It was hers. She was a great woman. Occasionally some of those pregnant women would have problems, and when anything went wrong during a birth, she would be blamed." At the same time, far-sighted Maria saw in advance that Trevignano would become a tourist haven for day trippers from Rome, and her intuitions helped to make the café a place of welcome. Ermete was thus the second generation to own his namesake café. When he was born in April 1928 in the old *borgo*, where he attended school, the town population was around 1,500, or almost the same as in the fourteenth century. In its early decades the café was mostly deserted during daytime.

"Every able-bodied man was hard at work all day," Ermete recollected. "Thanks to our good climate, and the soil rich with minerals, the people here were mostly farmers—some had come here from the Puglie and the Marches for the transhumance [summer transfer of livestock]. Some of these stayed on. Marrying into families here, they became farmers and lived off their crops, which they also sold to the towns nearby."

Boys as young as eight often worked in the fields, Ermete recounted. In springtime one of their tasks was to shoo away the magpies that pecked at seedlings. As a boy Ermete himself helped out at the town's olive press, the *frantoio*. Like most other Trevignano enterprises at that time, ownership of that press was a family affair, and it was eventually shared between Ermete and his cousin Nazzareno Avincola.

"We also had a boat and big fishnets, and from the time I was twelve I worked on our boat." He frowned: "While we were out fishing at night, hauling in those heavy nets, it would be bitterly cold!"

Shortly after the Second World War, Ermete would cycle to Vicarello to purchase milk, which he would resell to the village women. Almost all were dressed only in black, he recollected. The women did not enter the bar, it being guy territory, "So I sold the milk to them through a window."

The original café was the only source of amusement in the town. "We were the fulcrum of Trevignano. People came in of an evening to play cards and tell the same story over and over again." The café had no separate tables, but a *banco*, or single long table with benches. It was a plus that in the 1950s the café had one of the town's only three telephones. One was the property of the Carabinieri and the second, of the nearby Vicarello hot baths, then run by a German religious order. Thus Ermete's was the only telephone accessible to the public.

"Every big decision about the town was made in our café," said Ermete proudly. "Which means there were also plenty of confrontations," interjected with a smile his handsome youngest son Loris, who now manages the café and was accompanying me to the interview with his father, whose other sons are Costantino, born in 1955, and Fosco, born in 1958. In the Sixties a TV set was installed in the café. At the time it was the only one in town, or almost. "Everyone came to us to watch TV," Ermete recollected with pride.

Next, thanks to the economic "miracle" of the Sixties, which brought annual economic growth of 7 percent, Trevignano became a favorite of tourists. "It was our good luck to be close to Rome, and so countless Romans have been coming to us ever since," Ermete recalled during our interview. "We were lucky too in having good mayors."

An entire stretch of land known as "Il Possesso" was property of the town. When foreigners began arriving in the early Sixties, the then mayor, Carlo Cipollini, sold off the land at favorable prices. The fact that the buyer was obliged to build on the land within two years of purchase spurred construction, and hence the economy. Not least, the arrival of foreigners fostered a certain cosmopolitan attitude within the town earlier than elsewhere. "Mayor Cipollini understood progress," said Ermete approvingly.

As the café grew in popularity in the Sixties, it also grew in importance. However, it served no *cornetti*, for at that time the café had no bakery oven, and this was a problem. This Italian breakfast necessity had to be delivered all the way from Rome by "a certain Giorgio." But at last Ermete opened his own bakery in 1985. Ever since the *cornetti* have been Ermete's own—as they are now, along with mouth-watering pastries.

In celebration of the café's 80th anniversary on July 3, 2011, veteran journalist Paddy Agnew, who lives in Trevignano, wrote a paeon to Ermete's Café which ran in *The Irish Times* under the headline, "Bar saga mirrors 20th century Italy, from fascism to feminism."[60]

> The lovely evening, live traditional *transumanza* (shepherd) music and, above all, splendid and generous supplies of food and drink had ensured a full house. Ermete, who is still to be found working in the bar at six in the morning, sat at a long table in front of the bar, in the company of his wife, parish priest Don Carmelo and some of the village's elder citizens. As he sat there, the village paid a sort of homage, with

John O'Keeffe, portrait of Truman Peebles at 101 years of age, oil on canvas.

guests pushing their way through the madding crowd (there is nothing that quite so concentrates some folks as free grub) to shake hands and pay their respects. At the end of the night, a huge, absolutely delicious caramel and ice cream cake in the shape of the number 80 was produced, with Loris seemingly able to do a five loaves and two fishes act, with there being slices for everyone.

Ermete died in the summer of 2018. His son Loris and family carry on.

Another café that is part of Trevignano history is the Café La Vela. Along the waterfront, it is a long-time favorite of Ermete's friend, the American Truman Peebles, and of the artist and retired teacher John O'Keeffe. O'Keeffe, English, was teaching physical education in a school in Sheffield, in South Yorkshire, when an acquaintance mentioned that a British school in Rome, Saint George's, was looking for a phys ed teacher. "I'm your man," recalled O'Keeffe in a recent interview. "I signed on, finding a flat near the school." Truman's portrait, painted by O'Keeffe, hung on a wall at the Café La Vela for literally years. Long since retired from Saint George's, O'Keeffe and his wife Kay still spend part of every year in Trevignano, where he paints. "I've been painting since I was a child—I was interested in sports but also in painting, and I always did both. Once I painted a portrait of Judy Dench, who was very welcoming. It ended up in an exhibition."

These days O'Keeffe can often be found of a morning at Café La Vela, but it has become something of a long walk for Truman, who turned 108 years old in August of 2020 and lives alone in the *borgo* at this writing. Because Café Ermete is closer to his apartment, on many a morning Truman can be found seated there.

By evening Truman would walk to his favorite watering hole, the tiny pub then called Vini e Oli tucked inside a patch of medieval wall by roadside at the end of the borgo. To reach Vini e Oli (now Fuori le Mura), Truman had to descend a steep flight of steps from his little apartment midway through the *borgo* and make his way to its far end. To go home again he was sometimes accompanied as a courtesy by Ramona Roschini, the very pretty young woman who helped behind the counter at Vini e Oli, and who served Truman his daily single shot of Jack Daniels whiskey on ice.

For Truman, steps are a problem. Still, one evening in January 2016 Truman walked up two steep flights of stairs to attend a piano concert of classical music in the huge reception hall by the mayor's office. When the others in the audience realized he was there, they burst into applause, and the concert organizer, musicologist Angela Pardo, rushed after the concert to be photographed with him. To say that Truman is uniquely popular in Trevignano is an understatement. Truman's history begins in Harrington Park, New Jersey, where he was born August 26, 1912. When he was only seven, his mother died. As a teenager, along with other nature-loving youngsters, he frequented a little camp on a river near woodlands. The camp was run by an inspiring Roger Baldwin (1884–1981), cofounder in 1920 of the American Civil Liberties Union (ACLU) and its executive director for thirty years.

"I was just a boy when Roger Baldwin gave me a book by Thoreau. In it he wrote a little note, 'For Truman, my partner of the fields and woods,'" Truman recalled in one of our ten hours of interviews. Truman was just thirteen when Baldwin rose to fame for defending high school teacher Thomas Scopes in the famous "Monkey Trial" of 1925, when Scopes was tried for teaching evolution.

When Truman was sixteen, his carpenter father also died, and Roger Baldwin, by then the director of the ACLU, became Truman's legal guardian. In 1932, after graduation from Forest Ranger School in the Adirondack Mountains (a part of Syracuse University), Truman went to work for the Indian Service in Washington State as a timber cruiser, or woodlands surveyor, with the Yakima Indians. "My job was to go into woods and estimate how much marketable wood there was in the trees." From Washington State Truman was sent to New Mexico as a forester with the Soil Conservation Service. His role was to deal with the problems of land ownership between the Native Americans of the Pueblo tribe, who had been there for thousands of years, and the Spanish–Americans, who took over the land and assigned each Pueblo a little square patch of what had been their land. The job involved making a survey of how the Native Americans there lived, and to map some of the forests and see what use the Native Americans made of them.

When the Second World War began, the U.S. economy shifted on to a war footing. "The study of the woodlands on a Navajo reservation became immaterial," Truman recalled. As a result, he moved to Washington, DC, where he went to work for the Board of Economic Warfare. "The goal was to keep things running," said Truman. "This meant devising guidelines for banks, for money and for loans for postwar Italy and Yugoslavia."

At the end of the war, Truman served briefly in the the United Nations Relief and Rehabilitation Agency (UNRRA) for refugees. When this agency wound down, he transferred to the brand new United Nations Food and Agriculture Organization (FAO), created in 1945. When its headquarters were transferred from New York to Rome in 1951, Truman moved with them.

> I remember Rome in 1951—Those first impressions are important, but you forget them soon. Still, the only real difference with today was that it was dim: the available electricity was poor, and there were few street lights so you walked around at night seeing without seeing much. A great deal had to be rebuilt because the Germans deliberately destroyed much when they left, like the bridges in Florence, where they blew up one in the Arno River. The Florentines collected the pieces out of the water and rebuilt it.

In 1955, Truman took early retirement from the FAO, but stayed on in Rome, renting a room near the Colosseum for a time.

> But then I decided I wanted to get out of the city. I phoned my writer friend, Victor von Hagen, and told him I was in Rome and rethinking my future. Von Hagen said, "You're talking to the right person. You can live with me in Trevignano, pay minimal rent, share the kitchen, have your own bathroom, share expenses." And so I came to live with him, in his big house for a couple of years.
>
> On some days Victor was cheery and lots of fun, and some days sulky, telling me, "You don't do enough work in the house." He was really husky—he had been a boxer, and had big biceps, twice the normal size. Every once in a while he'd say, "Wanna trade punches?" I said no, I knew it would be the end of me. He had taught boxing at the University of Arizona and actually had a fight with "Cowboy" Jones, who knocked him flat, and that was the end of his boxing career.

At the time, author Von Hagen (1908–1985) was already famous, and working on a book on ancient roads. "Together for the book we explored the countryside, looking at old Roman roads." In the end that research contributed to two of Von Hagen's famous books, *Roman Roads* (1966) and *Roads that Led to Rome* (1967).

When Von Hagen decided to move to Arezzo in Tuscany, Truman remained in Trevignano, moving down into the town to stay with Nazzareno Avincola, who ran the Grotta Azzura restaurant on the waterfront around the corner from Café Ermete. The Trevignano world was small: the recently deceased Nazzareno was a cousin of Ermete.

> I first met Nazzareno through Victor von Hagen. We became close friends immediately and teamed up to work together on several projects. We grew Trevignano's first avocados, and then decided to raise chickens in a modern way. Most people in Trevignano raised chickens under very bad conditions.
>
> We built an up-to-date chicken house placed so as to receive maximum sunshine. We changed the place where eggs were hatched, creating a communal nest. Fresh water, proper fresh air, sunshine—all this made a difference. We successfully raised chickens both as laying hens and for meat. The result was that the eggs were clean—and kept Nazzareno's restaurant supplied with eggs.

By then Truman was getting on in years, though only anagraphically. In his early eighties he decided to study for a Ph.D. from the Fielding Graduate University in California. He elected psychology, focusing upon transactional analysis, or TA. This approach to psychoanalytic theory and therapy had been devised in the 1960s by psychiatrist Eric Berne, the author of *Games People Play*, which sold five million copies.

"I just drifted into it. I was always interested in people's problems, and at FAO I actually had done a bit of informal counselling," Truman ruminated. "We live by making transactions with other people and so, although the approach is not very popular now, it has a lot to say about how to make people more comfortable, and our own lives more comfortable."

In 1998 the town began what became an annual celebration of Truman's birthday with a street party in the *borgo*. For years after that the street fests continued, with a band playing and friends like the talented Penny Brown singing.

In later years Truman's younger son Patrick Peebles, an inventor, moved to Trevignano with his wife, Dikla, to be near his father. Older son Roger Peebles, a retired geohydrologist, and his wife Giovanna also began spending several months every year in town. For Truman,

> I like the life in Trevignano because everyone is so friendly. And it is very quiet, I can read or work and nobody bothers me. I just feel comfortable here. I think I like best the fact that I can remain by myself if I want to, and not be bothered by anyone else. And Trevignano today is not very different from then.
>
> The one thing I really dislike is the Italian bureaucracy!

Truman claims that Trevignano has changed fairly little in the past half century, save for the plethora of new buildings scrambling over the hillsides outside of the *borgo*.

What I probably like best about the Italians is their warmth. On the streets in Trevignano, they greet you—I don't know how many people I see who know me, though I don't always know them. They usually call me 'Druma', mispronouncing my name. Friendliness—I have a lot of friends and acquaintances here, they say hello, we sit in a café and talk. I feel comfortable here.

At the end of our interview sessions I asked Truman if he had a recipe for happiness.

Well, on happiness I have nothing to suggest, but I can tell you how I live. I eat like an animal, enjoying little snacks—small amounts of food—during the day, as nutritionist Adele Davis advised in her book *Let's Eat Well*. Music is a big part of my life, especially classical music, which I keep on all the time at home via internet: Chopin, Andras Schiff, the American composers. Not least, your learning should be lifelong.

19

Faith

Preacher, you want to pray?
If for me, do go right ahead

—Bracciano proverb

The earliest known evidence of faith on Lake Bracciano is the tubby, naked Mother Goddess, under two inches tall and carved of soapstone, found in the 8,000-year-old underwater village at the site known as La Marmotta, near Anguillara (see Chapter 4, "Twig brooms"). Underwater archaeologists diving down through 24 feet of water and 6 feet of mud found the tiny Venus placed, as if for a blessing, beneath the wood beam flooring of one of the Neolithic cottages which were abandoned, perhaps after an earthquake and/or fire, and subsequently submerged in the lake by a huge rise in the water level.

No one knows for sure, but the La Marmotta Mother Goddess appears to be far older than even that underwater Neolithic village. Speculation (and it can be no more than that) is that the Marmotta Venus was brought there by colonists arriving from the eastern Mediterranean, perhaps Thessaly. A ring indentation around her neck suggests that once the figure dangled from a string and was worn as a good-luck amulet, like the charms that dangle from the rear view mirrors of automobiles in today's Italy.

These mother goddesses were worshipped in remotest times as the givers of life and hence of rebirth, regeneration and agriculture. The body of La Marmotta's somewhat resembles the most famous of these, the Venus of Willendorf, found at the Austrian town of that name in 1908. Like that found at La Marmotta, the plump Willendorf goddess is tiny, at just over 4 inches high (11.1 cm). She is estimated to be 24,000 years old, dating from the Upper Paleolithic.

Other early signs of religiosity in Lake Bracciano appear in the votive offerings that were left at Vicarello, three miles from Trevignano, and thrown into the boiling springs in a fissure in the rocks to show gratitude to the gods (see Chapter 9, "Aqueductors"). The trove of ancient silver and silver-gilt cups and the occasional gold coin was discovered only in the mid-nineteenth century. Some are identified as dating from even before the Neolithic era, and hence demonstrate that the north shore of Lake Bracciano was inhabited or at least visited from earliest times.

Some of the later votive offerings rescued from that steaming fissure reflect the beliefs of the Etruscans, who settled in the first millennium BC on that same fertile, sun-drenched north shore of the lake at Trevignano. Other votive offerings, many dating from the eighth century BC, were also found in the hundreds of Etruscan tombs cut into the hillsides near the town. Not least, one cup found was covered with the names of every city from Cadiz to Vicarello, intimating that pilgrims had come from as far away as Spain; the votive cup was thus the equivalent of a map. (Some of today's scholars question this reading but offer little that is more convincing.)

To what deities would these votive offerings have been dedicated? One, from in or near Trevignano, was an engraved, gemstone-like oval of jasper (quartz) found around 1884 by a man known as "Guazzetti"; the exact date of the finding, the place and his full name are uncertain. It shows a god whose face has a hawk-like beak, and atop his head what looks like a rooster crest. The figure wears armor and holds in his left hand a shield and, in his right, a spear. His legs, splayed as if those of a merman, "terminate with the head of a snake or fish," archaeologist Elena Felluca wrote in the local magazine *Il Lago Sabatino*.[61]

Vertical lettering identifies the god as IANS SABATIAS. "The word Ians [Delta] Sabatias, or 'Of Janus of Sabazia', is written in characters somewhere between Greek and archaic Latin on the border of the stone," Felluca points out. Sabatia is the name of the lake and of the (presumed) lost ancient Roman city which, as is now believed, stood in front of today's Trevignano before being swallowed by the lake or destroyed by an earthquake.

The figure represented is clearly from the eastern Mediterranean and could represent the crest of the city of Sabazia, Felluca believes. Her theory is that this votive offering, to date unique, may have been an offering of thanks from one who survived the violent moment of passage from Etruscan to Roman control of the territory in the Fourth century BC.

Curiously, among the 160 known Etruscan deities and godlike heroes, who include a god of wolves and one of snakes, this is the only one bearing that name. Possibly it is an early version of the Roman god Janus, whose name was related to or derived from the Latin word *ianua*, meaning door or portal and hence beginnings; from it comes our month January. So Ians may have been a doorkeeper or protector, whose mermen legs referred to the lake. The shield he holds in his left hand and, in his right, a spear can be read as obvious symbols of power.

As for Sabatia, the original name of the lake, that word may derive from the name of the sky-father god Sabazios, worshipped by the Thracians and Phrygians. (The *-zios* at the end of the god's name derives from *dyeus*, precursor to the ancient Greek *Zeus* and Latin *deus*.)

Other scholars suggest that the name derives from Saturn or Sabus, the son of the god of sowing and hence of a farmer's well-being (the tribal name Sabines derives from this). "Sabatio was adored by his faithful with a cult expresssed through esoteric forms, whose initiations took place by night and had a sexual background; by day he was honored through chants and public processions," writes Maciucchi.[62]

A number of Etruscan divinities worshipped in and around Trevignano were similar to those in the rest of Southern Etruria. Among these was Nortia, the goddess of fate and chance, who became Fortuna under the Romans; a nail driven into a wall in her temple was part of an Etruscan new year fertility rite. Another popular deity in Etruria was Turan, the Etruscan goddess identified with the Greek Aphrodite and the Roman Venus; when called Turan Ati, she was the equivalent of the later Venus Genetrix.

Above: Saint Bernardino statue in annual Trevignano procession.

Left: Ians Sabatis, or Janus of Sabazia: possibly the crest of ancient Roman city at Trevignano.

Ancient Roman statue of Apollo discovered in Vicarello hot springs in 1977.

After the territory at Trevignano's neighboring Vicarello with its hot springs was conquered by the Romans, its principal shrine was dedicated to the god Apollo, divinity of medicine and healing, and the springs and shrine named the *Termae Apollinares ad lacus Sabatinum*. During an excavation there in 1977 the finding of the torso of a statue of a youthful Apollo wearing a cloak tossed over his shoulders caused a sensation. It has been dated to around AD 130 or during the reign of the Emperor Hadrian, but some experts believe it is considerably older. If complete the statue would have stood some six feet tall. Restored, it is now the centerpiece of the small, elegant archaeological museum at Bracciano. Although much damaged by the hot springs, archaeologists point out that it resembles the Apollo Belvedere inside the Vatican, which also has a shawl-like cloak draped over his shoulder.

In the mid-eighteenth century, when the baths were the property of German monks, a gleaming cup was noticed in the gash in the rocks from which gushed boiling hot water. Workmen were sent into the water to retrieve items and coins—and emerged burnt. But they found votive cups which, among others, gave thanks to Aesculapius, the son of Apollo, god of medicine and healing. Other Roman-era cups found there were offerings to lesser deities and to Silvanus, god of the forest (a Vicarello cup dedicated to Silvanus is now in the National Roman Museum).

A particularly fascinating find in the hot springs was a gilded silver cup showing the Greek god Pan. The satyr depicted was deemed so vulgar that the Vatican, proprietors of Vicarello, declined to keep the cup; put on the market it wound up in the Cleveland Museum of Art, where I had the delight of seeing it.

In Trevignano itself, there was at least one important Roman temple. Its whereabouts are lost, but its importance is indicated by the impressive white marble panel set in the grass in the main piazza facing the town hall. No one knows exactly where that panel comes from.

Another important church in Trevignano is the tiny church of Santa Caterina, built in the late sixteenth century. Snuggled against a wall of the town hall, it actually occupies one wing of an early, larger Roman building, dating from the Third or Fourth century AD. Its construction, primarily in *opus reticulatum,* or square blocks of the local volcanic rock basalt worked in a diamond pattern, is typical of late ancient Rome, and visible in numerous buildings at Pompeii. On either side of the (much later) doorway are two arches, perhaps indicating that the building had served as a market in Roman times.

The building became an early Christian church, named for Santa Caterina, which was restored in 1620, but then abandoned for centuries. By the altar is a sixteenth century fresco showing St. Catherine of Alexandria enthroned together with St. Sebastian and St. Rocco.

Trevignano's most imposing church is devoted to the Assumption of the Blessed Virgin Mary, or Santa Maria Assunta, which rises from the steep hillside between the ruins of the hilltop fortress and the old *borgo* below. It was built by the Orsini princes, who at that time still owned both the Bracciano castle and Trevignano, in the early sixteenth century on the site of an earlier Gothic church. Supposedly they built it in thanks for Trevignano's stout defense in 1496 against the Borgia pope, whose army had destroyed the Trevignano fortress but, which contributed to the Borgias' defeat at Bracciano.

A century after the church was built it was restructured and given an imposing bell tower. To this day that tower evokes interest because it is, it seems, the sole surviving

Silver cup found in the Vicarello hot springs, now in the Cleveland Art Museum.

20

A Lake at Risk

Curse, and you will be cursed

—Bracciano proverb

The collected postcards in these pages are an attempt to sketch a biography of Lake Bracciano and some of its fascinating inhabitants over time. One of these was the late historian Ofelio Maciucchi, whose writings I have often quoted in these pages. He happened to be the father of today's mayor of Trevignano, the attractive Claudia Maciucchi, in her early fifties. She is definitely a Trevignano native with a background: in the early eighteenth century her businessmen forebears migrated from Venice to settle first at Cività Castellana, northeast of Rome near the Tiber River, and then in Trevignano. For over a decade Maciucchi, who was trained as a lawyer, worked along with her brother Massimo in his law firm. Then, in a hard-fought battle in June 2016, this mother of twins and wife of a busy restaurateur was elected the town's first female mayor. "What my father taught me and my brother was to love this town," she said in an interview in her office in the town hall shortly after her installation.

Among the most vexing problems she has faced—she and the mayors of the other two towns on the lake, Bracciano and Anguillara—is the endangered lake. Historical Lake Bracciano, celebrated as one of Italy's most beautiful and least polluted, comes with a peculiarity. Probably because of its volcanic origins and earthquakes, from time to time over many thousands of years its water level has risen drastically. One of these sudden surges literally drowned the Neolithic town known as La Marmotta, which was rediscovered in the 1980s beneath deep water and a thick layer of mud, as we saw in Chapter 4, "Twig Brooms." During the Bronze Age the waters again rose radically, submerging at least five villages scattered on what were then the lake shores. A few hundred years later the important ancient Roman town of Sabatia was similarly submerged, as were luxurious lakeside villas built in the age of Marcus Aurelius on the northern lake shore near Trevignano.

Lake Bracciano has long warranted official protection both as the centerpiece of the 64-square-mile Regional Park of Bracciano–Martignano, and also because it serves as an important emergency source of water for Rome itself. For reasons of public health, it is circled by an efficient sewer system, and the purity of its water is regularly tested.

To avoid pollution, fishermen, and only those with licenses, must use, not gas-powered, but electric motors. Otherwise the sole motorboats permitted on Lake Bracciano are those belonging to the paramilitary Carabinieri police. A single tourist ferryboat, equipped with a café, is also allowed to transit, calling in at all three towns.

Although its cone tilts slightly, making the lake deepest at the north, or along the Trevignano–Vicarello coastline, its normal depth varies between 12 and 16 meters (40 and 53 feet). Its maximum depth is of 164 meters (538 feet), while its central area plunges below sea level by 1 meter (just over 3 feet).

But times changed. In the springtime of 2017 the water level sank by 1.22 meters (4 feet) below "hydrometric zero", or the surface elevation level as established by the geologists of the regional park authority. Continuing to sink, by summertime it had dropped to 1.8 m, or almost 6 feet below hydrometric zero—twice the normal annual drop in the water level during the past half century. The solitary tourist ferryboat was unable to approach the dock at Trevignano until autumn of 2018, and even then unable to dock at Bracciano.

With its rich volcanic soil and gentle climate, Trevignano has been a fertile farming center for centuries. When rainfall was poor, the farmers often irrigated fields and greenhouses with lake water drawn from boreholes drilled—many illegally—down 150 feet or more below the surface. Some still do.

"That loss could be cut in half with improved technology," said Professor Riccardo Valentini, climatologist at the Tuscia University in Viterbo, former researcher at the Carnegie Institution in Stanford, California. "The irrigation is overdone. It's like overfeeding a child. You feed them too much just in case."

The consequences are extremely serious. "This level of stress has not been seen in centuries," according to botanist Mattia Azella of La Sapienza Rome University. "The lake is unique in Europe as a habitat for vegetation, with seventeen species of underwater plants, some extremely rare." The severe drop in the water level means that those underwater plants closest to the shore which feed the fish are left to dry and die, Azella explained. These underwater plants are particularly interesting because of the volcanic nature of the lake, whose rocky substrata has a strong influence on the cleanliness of the lake and favors the growth of plants as well as fish. The receding of the water means that the shoreline plants push inward, where the water bed is already crowded. The plants die, and hence the food for the fish disappears, as do the fish.

Bird life too is affected. In the two-year period 2000–2002 a census showed that the lake hosted no less than ten thousand aquatic birds. Some lay eggs on little floating nests near or just on the shoreline. "But as the shoreline recedes, foxes, rats and people too seize their eggs," said botanist Azella. In addition, the cleansing effect of the denitrification of lake water—which occurred naturally in the lake—is also being lost. Denitrification, or the conversion of nitrates (NO3) to inert nitrogen gas (N2), is the removal of excess nitrate from groundwater contaminated by the over-use of fertilizers.

In past centuries, Lake Bracciano was fed by the water from three other lakes situated upon slightly higher terrain east of Trevignano, through underground streams known as aquifers. The largest of the three was in the Valle del Baccano, itself a vast volcanic crater. However, that lake was drained in the mid-nineteenth century to create more farmland, in what was then considered a far-sighted, modernizing agricultural venture. The second

Drastically receding water level widens the beach area—and shows lake itself at risk.

Across lake from Trevignano, receding water at Bracciano dock, June 2017.

lake, very small, dried up on its own. One lake remains to feed into Bracciano: the tiny Lake Martignano, which may itself be at risk.

The primary source for lake renewal thus remains atmospheric: the rainwater that flows down from the hills and into the lake and from the myriad underground springs which underlie the territory. These springs send bubbles surging up to the lake surface, where they are readily visible and even felt underfoot while wading in the water. "In the past rainwater regularly compensated for the lowering of the water level," says Rolando Luciani, past president of the lake consortium, composed of representatives of the three townships and of the Lazio region. "But the lake no longer follows that natural cycle. And simply because this had never happened before, we have no measures in place to deal with it."

The implications for the future were discussed at a conference on the lake held at Anguillara Sabazia on March 11, 2017, where concerned hydrologists, environmentalists and geologists analyzed the risks. As one geologist there explained, "Lake Bracciano has always had oscillations, but in recent decades never more than one meter (3 feet) a year. Moreover, what is frightening is that the drop in the water level actually took place in wintertime." Global warming is worsening the situation, he added: "With warm weather and more sunlight, evaporation will increase."

Another particularly grievous problem is pollution of the ground water that flows from the hills into the lake—the underground aquifers—from the use of chemical fertilizer on the sprawling acres of hazelnut trees that are tending to replace the traditional crops like grapevines. In addition, herbicides are spread beneath the trees to avoid the growth of weeds that hinder collection of the hazelnuts.

Much of the water being sent to thirsty Rome from the lake is lost, seeping out of the crumbling aqueducts. Most estimate that loss at 40 percent; for Deputy Mayor Galloni it is 44 percent. Moreover, by the time the water reaches Rome another 8,000 liters (2,113 gallons) a second are lost due to negligent maintenance of the pipes that underlie the Eternal City. In short, if 40 percent is lost *en route*, that same amount or more disappears into the underground morass of the city itself.

To fight back on behalf of the lake, a citizens' action committee called Comitato di Difesa del Bacino Lacuale Bracciano-Martignano was created in early 2017. In their first report they wrote that, "The reduction of the volume of available water within the lake ecosystem is the result of a subtle form of stress." No rejoicing if enlarged beaches result; they may seem to bring "temporary tourism advantages"—but tourism overload can itself damage the environment.

Already, given the concentration of pollutants, the arsenic level of lake water has risen to *circa* 85 micrograms per liter, or well above limits permitted, says the committee report, while sewage waste treatment, the responsibility of the public water company Acea Ato2, is insufficient. Concentrated, the pollutants converge to flow into the Arrone River near Anguillara Sabazia, the sole natural outlet of the lake. Because the Arrone water is used *en route* for irrigating fields and watering herds, any degrading of the quality of the water harms both crops and animals. Along the way some of the lake water is also wasted.

In the 1600s a dam had been built near the source of the Arrone in hopes of keeping the lake water level stable. Five locks were added, but all are now broken. When the lake water level is low, as recently it has been, the once navigable Arrone turns bone dry.

plants and animals can be found nowhere else in the world, and it was once famed for having the purest water on the planet. Today about 30 percent of its area is endangered: according to the *Siberian Times,* and its water is unsafe for both animals and humans to drink.

By 2007 the Aral Sea by southwestern Kazakhstan had shrunk to 10 percent and seemed close to disappearing, partly due to Soviet Union decisions to divert its water into irrigation projects. For *The Daily Telegraph*, this is "one of the planet's worse environmental disasters."[67] Fortunately, efforts in recent years to replenish it via new dams have been at least partly successful.

In Italy itself, Lake Tagliamento in the mountainous Friuli was described by *La Repubblica* daily on April 14, 2017, as "a long stretch of sand from which by night the tractors arrive to steal the pebbles." Behind this, according to local sources, was the dry autumn of 2015, which meant that the rainfall in the nearby mountains that autumn was 40 percent less than normal. Other lakes running dry in Italy include Lakes Mis, Sauris, Resia and Santa Giustina.

The shriveling of Lake Bracciano is thus not hypothetical. Climate change, reckless irrigation, illegal deep wells, chemical pollution, neglected maintenance, bureaucratic sloth, and an excessive amount of water siphoned away for Roman consumption (and for profit)—all these bedevil the lake. An obvious conclusion is that the problems are so many-layered that to confront them has become complex, to the point that those responsible for action face such a tremendous challenge that they can and do readily find excuses to avoid dealing with them. The worse the situation, the less willing to face it are those responsible for it.

At this writing the situation shows a slight improvement, fortunately, thanks to the at least temporary reduction in Acea's withdrawal of lake water after the loud protests, together with the unexpectedly heavy rainfalls in the late summer and early autumn of 2018 and 2019. In a single day in October 2018, abundant rainfall helped rise the lake water by 3 inches within just twenty-four hours. "The lake is beginning to breathe," commented Mattia Azzella that Oct. 6. However, without systematic research accompanied by systematic action, this modest attempt at a biography of a Roman lake risks becoming an obituary for the lake, its history, its ancient treasures, its life, which is to say our life.

Meanwhile life does go on, and especially business life. In July of 2019 a headline proclaimed that "The Chinese buy Lake Bracciano." This is not quite accurate: a Chinese group did *not* buy the entire lake; they bought the the almost 2,511-acre area of the ancient baths at Vicarello, which, albeit physically closer to Trevignano, fall under the jurisdiction of the City of Bracciano. The Chinese business group, which already owns a successful spa complex in France, purchased the Vicarello estate for a reported €25 million ($28 million); elsewhere the price was given as €16 million.

The baths *(terme)* with their natural hot water springs were developed for healing purposes by a German religious order in the eighteenth century, and a four-story building with rooms for patients added the following century. During the Second World War German troops occupied the building as a hospital.

The new owners' plans for demolition of the old hotel and its reconstruction into a luxury establishment that would attract rich tourists have reportedly been discussed. However, by one account the famous springs now produce only a limited amount of hot

At Vicarello baths, abandoned nineteenth-century four-story building.

water, so the question arises as to whether they will be allowed to drill the land in search of new hot water sources. Environmentalists believe that this will not be permitted.

A serious problem, in addition, is the famous Casina Valadier, a hunting lodge on the edge of the Vicarello property but divided from it by a more modern road. The building stands atop ancient Roman foundations upon which the Orsini built a hunting lodge in 1500, and which was then rebuilt in 1789 by the famous Italian architect Giuseppe Valadier. Both the Casina Valadier and the adjacent tiny church, which dates from 1753, are abandoned and crumbling into ruins. Until a few decades ago the entire Vicarello property still belonged to the German church, but in 1991 was taken over by the British-based multinational Schroders, an investment bank that planned to build there a swanky golf course surrounded by country houses. After successful protests from environmental groups, the Italian government placed restrictions upon the territory's development, and the bank and its international investors were eventually obliged to back away. Will history repeat itself? Stay tuned.

21

Flight

Rags always soar
High into the air

—Bracciano proverb

Heading into Rome one day via the train from Trevignano's neighbor, Anguillara, I shared a seat with a man carrying a gigantic falcon in a cage. I was not particularly surprised: just as I had, the falconer had come from Trevignano. The village is home to many a colorful bird on beach and in the water, not to mention the swans, but in addition it most unusually hosts the *Centro Volo Rapaci*, or Center for Birds of Prey. Located above the town on a slope of the Rocca Romana, the Center, open most weekends, is a favorite of youngsters. In its eleven-acre park visitors can learn about birds of prey—falcons, owls, eagles and more besides—under the watchful eyes of expert falconers, beginning with park director, Paola Falcone (her real name). Here the youngsters (and not only they) hear lectures, see the falconers feed the trained birds, and watch the birds in flight. Visitors can feed themselves as well: in the Center's sprawling grounds is a picnic area with, on offer, a simple menu of traditional or vegetarian grilled sausages and potatoes, all roasted on a wood fire.

Falconry dates back to earliest times in the Middle East and Mongolia. It was a means of obtaining food by using trained birds of prey to capture quarry. In Italy it became particularly famous under the medieval emperor Frederick II, who built castles throughout the Italian south and lived in a grandiose one in Puglie. Frederick was the author of *De Arte Venandi cum Avibus* (On the Art of Hunting with Birds), *c.* 1240. Still considered a masterpiece of ornithology, Frederick is said to have worked on it for thirty years.

From that time on to hunt with falcons was a European status symbol. It became the exclusive pursuit of aristocrats, who organized elaborate hunting parties. Maintaining the birds was costly; the most skillful birds were worth more than their weight in gold. *The Book of St. Albans*, printed in 1486, informs us that the typical punishment for what was then called "hawking" was to cut off the hands of "people who kept birds above their social rank, which also served as an excellent deterrent to the crime."[68] The presumed author Dame Julyans Barnes (also known as Juliana Berners) explains the hierarchy of individuals and birds. Depending upon his social class, a man (and one woman of the fourteen listed) was entitled to a particular bird. The emperor's was the eagle; the baron's, a buzzard; the squire's, a lanner falcon, and the lady's, the merlin. This European falconry elitism endured until gunpowder came into common use in the eighteenth century, and rendered the sport anachronistic. Today the sport is back, although without hands being chopped off; and falconry clubs are scattered throughout the U.S. as well as Europe; one posh resort in Tuscany offers a three-day course in falconry.

Trevignano's Center on the Rocca Romana also offers courses, but its star attraction is Olga, a huge and remarkably likeable foundling eagle around fifty years of age. Originally from Russia, Olga was discovered around 1990 in a little town near Salerno. She had been one of many originally there, but all the others disappeared—whether stolen, killed or eaten is unknown. The sole survivor, Olga was captured and locked in a small cage behind stout iron bars. Seeking freedom, she banged her body against the iron bars. Even her beak was ruined, to the point that, when bits of meat were on offer, she was unable to grab them. In this way she subsisted mostly on straw.

"She was more dead than alive—terrorized, slamming her body against the cage walls, and nearly starved," relates Falcone. "Doing this ruined her beak, leaving her unable to feed herself."

Falcone managed to acquire the eagle. The next step was to repair the damage to her health. From Rome, she contacted in Milan Italy's sole veterinarian specialized at that time in big birds. The veterinarian trimmed Olga's ruined beak as if giving a manicure. "Just like a fingernail, the beak slowly grew back. And finally Olga was able to eat!" Falcone exclaimed.

"Next we had to strengthen her muscles so that she could fly again." It was a slow process. Six months passed before Falcone and her fellow big bird enthusiasts in Trevignano could begin to reteach Olga to fly. "We would run down the hillside with tempting food hoping that, one day, she would fly by herself." Finally one day a thermal current helped lift Olga skyward. After soaring 1,500 feet into the air, she returned safely.

Although she is now elderly and no longer flies at all, Olga has remained in good health. She has appeared on a popular Italian nationwide TV show and, more recently, at a talk on birds of prey held in the Trevignano town hall. Speakers were Falcone herself, Polish trainer Bogdan Las, who caressed the bird throughout the event, and Alessandra Raeli, an expert in "*guferia*" or owlery. That word may be unfamiliar to those of a certain age, but not to Harry Potterites, for it happens to be the name of a room at the top of the west Tower of Hogwarts Castle where the school's and the students' pet owls were housed.

Besides offering flight demonstrations and courses in falconry, the Center offers excursions and classes in photographing falcons and owls. Another focus is care for the natural environment, which involves lessons on "herbology," or herbalism, the medicinal uses of plants. This is a Harry Potter popularity derivative, as well as a theme seriously enough regarded that the Royal Botanic Garden of Edinburgh offers a diploma in the subject.

Eagles, owls and swans are not the sole flying creatures on Lake Bracciano. Directly across the lake from Trevignano at Vigna di Valle is Italy's most important air museum,

Owl expert Alessandra Raeli and feathered friend Costanza, Centro Volo Rapaci, Trevignano Romano.

Olga the Eagle with Paola Falcone and Bogdan Las at falconry lecture, Trevignano town hall.

the Museo Storico Aeronautica Militare, operated by the Italian Air Force. Located in a lakefront seaplane station that dates from 1904, it is the third oldest such museum in the world, and its four giant hangars sprawl over 3.2 acres. From here the first Italian hot-air military balloon was launched in 1908. Inside the hangars are aircraft, a library, and exhibits that document the history of aviation, and Italy's crucial role. All but one of the airplanes and helicopters on view are authentic. Among them are two gliders, forty-four aircraft with propellers, and twenty jet aircraft, plus seventeen piston and three jet engines, there to be seen and studied. A Canadair fighter plane dates from 1947; Canadair planes still draw water regularly from Lake Bracciano to quench the all too frequent summer fires, but also to teach aspiring pilots how to graze over the water so as to fill the tanks and then return aloft.

A singular exhibition that would be easy to ignore is merely a stretch of fabric dangling from behind a glass partition. It happens to be a vestige of the oldest aircraft that existed. If air history begins in Italy with Leonardo Da Vinci, in modern times it begins with the development of the hot-air balloon. The very first of these was made in France in 1783 by the brothers Joseph and Jacques Montgolfier, after noticing that a sealed empty paper bag went afloat above a fire. No sooner had they built and tested one than Europe was swept with fascination with the building and flying of what was

Seaplane station created in 1908 on Lake Bracciano at Vigna di Valle shown here in the First World War, now a museum. (*Photo courtesy Museo Storico Vigna di Valle*)

was echoed and amplified in their often abstract depictions of planes and parachutes hurtling through space.

The Futurist Movement officially ended in 1944, but in recent years has regained popularity, and the first comprehensive U.S. exhibition on Futurism took place in New York's Guggenheim Museum in 2014. Aeropainting was a major theme: in the words of the exhibition catalogue, "Propelled by Italy's military preeminence in aviation, the [Futurists'] fascination with the machine shifted focus from the automobile to the airplane."[70] The following year an aeropainting exhibition was mounted inside the Colosseum in Rome, and the private Galleria Russo showed sixty works by Tato including the stunning "Flying Over the Coliseum in a Spiral" (1930).

Another unexpected exhibit is the embalmed body of a 10-inch tall fox terrier. The sight was startling: just what was an embalmed dog doing in a museum of aeronautical history? But then I noticed a card saying, "Donation of the Nobile family." It turned out that that this was Titina, the beloved foundling pet of Umberto Nobile (1885–1978), the Roman aeronautical engineer, pilot and explorer. Nobile had found the dog on a Roman street, abandoned and starving, in 1925. Shortly afterward, with the Norwegian Roald Amundsen and a crew of Italians and Norwegians, Nobile successfully designed and flew the *Norge* over the North Pole on May 12, 1926. Nobile would go nowhere without Titina, and for that flight, believed to be the first in history, Titina wore an Italian tricolor sash of red, white and green. She also gained fame for barking away a polar bear. Following the successful flight of the *Norge*, Titina accompanied Nobile on a celebrity tour that took them to New York and Washington. There, when Nobile was received by President Calvin Coolidge, Titina peed on a White House carpet.

Two years later Nobile designed and flew another dirigible, the *Italia*. That purely scientific expedition, financed by the City of Milan, departed Milan on April 15. After crossing the pole three times the flight ended in tragedy on May 25 when the airship suddenly lost altitude and crashed on polar ice. Out of the crew of sixteen, just nine, including Nobile, severely injured with broken arm and broken leg, survived the crash, as did Titina. The survivors had supplies: although the airship flew away, wreckage of its gondola lay in the snow. Hoping for rescue, the crew raised a tent which they smeared with red dye to make it visible. The red dye was aboard the plane for making hydrological measurements beneath the surface of the ice.

Thus began what is described as the "largest and most comprehensive" rescue effort the world had yet seen. It succeeded after thirty-one days because petty officer second class Giuseppe Biagi, the sole radio operator on the expedition, managed to recover the transmitter, receiver and enough batteries to last sixty hours.[71] From aluminum salvaged from the wrecked control cabin Biagi devised an antenna. When Biaggi picked up the first functioning radio signal, he gave a shout. The other survivors were thrilled—until he admitted that he'd shouted because he'd heard that a favorite soccer team had won.[72]

Twelve days later a Russian amateur radio operator picked up his signal. Still, it was altogether a month after the crash when a rescue plane found the red tent. Because that small aircraft could carry only one passenger, Nobile, the most severely injured, was the first to leave, taking with him Titina. Another eighteen days passed before the others were rescued. In Fascist Italy, and not only there, the fact that the commander left before the crew brought him endless accusations of cowardice, and crowds in Norway yelling "Death to Nobile!" One Norwegian newspaper called Nobile a "jester whose insane enterprise was the cause of the whole tragedy." Nobile came under attack in Italy from Marshal Italo Balbo, among others, and resigned from the air force. For several years he taught in the United States at the Lewis College of Aviation, Science and Technology in Lockport, Illinois, returning to Italy after 1943 and the fall of Fascism. In 1945 he was rehabilitated, and the story of the red tent became the subject of numerous books and movies. One, *The Red Tent*, made from a book Nobile wrote in 1967, was an Italian–Soviet co-production of 1969 starring Sean Connery, Claudia Cardinale, Hardy Kruger and Peter Finch as Nobile.

Besides the embalmed Titina, in the museum is a display of drawings and photographs of the *Norge*, with their specifications and technical details. Centerpiece is the original radio set from the *Italia*, which saved the lives of the survivors. In a commemoration organized by radio operator Biagi's grandson, Giuseppe Biagi, the *Italia* expedition of ninety years before was held in May, 2018, in the museum, and attended by descendants of the survivors. I was among those fortunate to attend.

In the museum is just one model airplane, rather than the original, but it is of special interest. In 1903 near Kitty Hawk, North Carolina, the brothers Wilbur and Orville Wright managed to keep aloft for fifty-nine seconds a flying machine they had built with a 16-horsepower motor. Within just three years the Wrights' heavier-than-air "Flying Machines" were sufficiently perfected that they were granted Patent Number 821,393, and the U.S. Army ordered six. In 1908 the Wrights took a ship to Europe to negotiate with the French, who were seeking a license to build their own Flying Machines. The Wrights' sample plane had already arrived, but had been damaged in shipment, and Wilbur spent two nervous months repairing it for flight. In the event all went well. The following April the brothers and Orville's wife Katherine traveled onward to Italy, to the Centocelle quarter on the outskirts of Rome. As in France, their flight demonstrations there attracted huge crowds, and, for the first time in history, a film was made showing scenes from their aircraft in flight. Visible on YouTube, it is an amazing spectacle.[73]

At Centocelle King Victor Emmanuel III attended the flight demonstrations, and the Wrights gave flying lessons to Italian military pilots Lieutenants Mario Calderara and Umberto Savoia. Later the Wrights donated to Italy their plane, the fourth manufactured in France. Although that donated airplane is lost, its original motor, still functional, is on view in the museum at Vigna di Valle, along with a model of the plane they flew in Italy.

Another military plane that made history was the S.I.T. Blériot XI-2 that was flown in Libya by Italian pilots in 1911 and 1912. At that time Italy was at war with Turkey, and the battles were fought in Libya. It was the first time in the history of warfare that an air force participated with an army. The aircraft were still fragile, but they began with reconnaissance missions, taking the first photographs of enemy troops and dropping, onto the terrified enemy, the grapefruit-sized bombs.

These first missions with bombardments from the sky were reported worldwide in the press. With the Blériot, Italy "set the record for being the first country to use aircraft in an offensive operation," writes historian Mondini.[74] "The flights showed the war zones and revealed the oases where the enemy was located in force, their rear lines and even the bunkers hidden among the desert dunes."

With the beginning of the First World War, air bombardments and surveillance flights became the order of the day. The Italians played a prominent role, for they had produced the trimotor airplane, the Caproni.

Fiorello La Guardia (1882–1947), an Italian immigrant who later became the mayor of New York, entered the fledgling U.S. Army Air Service as a lieutenant and later became the commander of the hundred or so American pilots in Italy. For Major La Guardia, for whom a New York airport was later named, the tri-motor Caproni bombers, in service on the border with Austria, were superior to all others.

By coincidence, prior to this in 1916, my grandfather Major Alfred Wilson Harris, architect and pioneer aviator, had disassembled and shipped, in containers, American-made aircraft to Paris, where he had the planes reassembled and set up an air field. This became inefficient, and in Major La Guardia's time, the U.S. decided to take over a Caproni factory and make use of these excellent Italian planes. Grandfather Major Harris was dispatched by the U.S. government to the factory in Milan to oversee production there of the bombers on order for America's proto-air force. Working together with France and Britain, all told 3,650 biplanes and triplanes were produced there.

The Caproni series had been designed by Engineer Giovanni Battista (Gianni) Caproni in 1913 and first flown in 1914, the year before Italy entered the war. A graduate of the Munich Polytechnic in 1907, Caproni became fascinated with aviation after seeing one of the Wright brothers' demonstrations. Poet Gabriele D'Annunzio had also been inspired by Wilbur Wright, with whom he had flown in 1909. D'Annunzio flew a Caproni in raids over Assling and Chapavano, and bombed the naval base at Cattaro. In a flying accident during that war, he lost an eye.

The Caproni Ca. 100 at the Vigna di Valle museum, produced in 1928 and used for training pilots, is a single-engine biplane made of wood and fabric. Later Capronis had three engines; a bomber, it was particularly large for its time.

During the Second World War, Furio Lauri (1918–2002) was enrolled in the 368th Squadron of the 151st Autonomous CT Group. In the early years of the war, pilot Lauri saw combat in Italy, Libya and Tunisia. But on September 8, 1943, an armistice between Italy and the Allies split Italy in two. It was the end of Fascism. From that time on Lauri fought against Italy's previous allies, the Germans, including in Rome at Porta San Paolo. Countless Italian soldiers had remained trapped behind the newly drawn lines and sought refuge in the mountains north of Rome. Many of those captured by the Reich military were slaughtered for allegedly betraying the alliance. A goodly number of those supporting the Allies became partisan fighters. Flying a Fieseler monomotor Storch produced in Germany, Lauri rescued fallen airmen from behind the German lines. The Storch—which the Italians called "the Stork"—needed only 120 feet for takeoff and could land on a strip just 60 feet long. In a daring mountain rescue in April 1945 Lauri saved the lives of two wounded British officers, who were taking part in a secret operation organized by the British together with Italian partisan fighters. For this Italy awarded him its Gold Medal of Valor. The Fieseler Fi. 156 Storch which Lauri flew for that rescue is on view in the aeronautics museum at Vigna di Valle.

The courageous aviator Furio Lauri is credited as founder of the Scuola di Volo Club Arrow, a flying school for ultra-light aircraft that is located directly across Lake Bracciano from the aeronautics museum, which is to say behind Trevignano, *en route* to Sutri and the Via Cassia.

President of the Club Arrow since the year 2000 is Nando Gambini, who, in a meeting at the Club Arrow, told me of its founder Lauri's extraordinary life. Gambini is both military and civilian parachutist, and a passionate delta planist with over 180 hours of free flight. Since 1999 he has been an instructor in sports flying, and in 2001 participated in the prestigious Schneider Cup race for ultra-lights. He pilots a Sky Arrow 450 T and directs the flying school and examines candidates. Gambini also explained that the club was initially located at Fiano Romano, some twenty miles distant, but had transferred to the sprawling fields near Trevignano just ten years ago. With eighty-five members, the club today has a fleet of four ultra-light biplanes. Three are Italian-made SkyArrow with tandem-seats; its wings atop the body of the plane permit maximum visibility to pilot and passenger. The fourth ultra-light sports plane, with seats side by side, is the Technam P96, made in Naples, which has low wings. All weigh under 450 kilos (990 pounds).

And now, after visiting falconry and air museum, my turn to take flight was approaching. Enzo Merlina is a journalist-photographer colleague and friend living in Trevignano. He was summoned from Milan to Rome by another of our colleagues, Dennis Redmont, at the time director of Associated Press. At AP Merlina became chief photo editor. "I've always loved flying," he told me as we chatted by the Club Arrow landing strip. "When I was a little boy in Milan my mother took me to see planes taking off and landing at the Linate airport. It left me with a passion for flight."

Now approaching seventy, Merlina was age sixty-seven when, one morning in the Café La Vela in Trevignano, he chanced to see a leaflet mentioning the Club Arrow flight school. He decided on the spot that he wanted to learn to fly, and promptly enrolled. After thirty-four hours of flight with an instructor he flew his own first solo flight. "Because of my age it took a bit longer to pass my flying test," he said. We clambered into one of the Club's Sky Arrow planes and readied for take-off. "Did you prepare your last will and testament?" an onlooker joked.

Down the long, long grassy runway we raced, and at the end the plane took off. We were airborne. Into my earphones came Merlina's voice, saying, "We have to stay above the electric wire lines." Well, yes. Passing over rolling fields elegantly planted with grape vines and hazelnut trees in severe rows, we reached the lake shore, to hover for a moment over Trevignano. Then, coasting along the shoreline, we continued to the Bracciano Castle, surprisingly (to me) in the shape of a huge triangle; from the road it appears a square. After a half hour or so we turned back, again over the lake shore, toward the tiny airstrip. Friends later asked if the flight had been frightening. No, it was not.

But during that marvelous half hour I came to understand what had happened. For just a brief moment in time I had become one of the swans hovering over my lake.

Taking off: journalist-photographer and hobby pilot Enzo Merlina, with your author.

Endnotes

1 Most proverbs that introduce chapters are from Angela Carlino Bandinelli, *Parlando di Bracciano...*, (Roma: Edizioni Mediterranee, 1989), p. 162.
2 Nassim Nicholas Taleb, *The Black Swan* (New York: Random House; London: Penguin, 2007, 2010).
3 Pasquale Tridente, Preface Antonella Morichelli, *Trevignano Ieri ed oggi*, Comune di Trevignano Romano, 2010, town history 1900–1920.
4 *Ibid.*
5 Ida Caruso, "Lake Bracciano: the historic landscape," Trevignano Romano Museo Civico e Area Archaeologica, Comune di Trevignano, 2002. Caruso is with the Soprintendenza per i Beni-Archeologici dell'Etruria Meridionale.
6 Yuval Noah Harari, *Sapiens, A Brief History of Humankind* (London: Vintage, 2011).
7 "Stocking the Paleolithic Pantry," *Archaeology*, Vol 57 No 5, Sept/Oct 2004.
8 Caruso, *op. cit.*
9 Radomir Tichy, "The Earliest Maritime Voyaging in the Mediterranean: View from the Sea", *Zivà Archeologie REA* 18/2016.
10 Nicholas J. Saunders, *The Poppy: A History of Conflict, Loss, Remembrance, and Redemption* (London: Oneworld Publications, 2013), p. 6. Also see http://www.livescience.com/49666-prehistoric-humans-psychoactive-drugs.html
11 Giulio Bigazzi, Giovanna Radi, Massimo Odone, "The Italian Obsidian sources," *Archeometriai Muhely*, Jan. 2005, pp. 1-11.
12 Jane Brody, "Is the Paleo Diet Right for You?," *New York Times*, Aug. 6, 2018.
13 Rebecca Rupp, "Prehistoric Dining: The Real Paleo Diet," *National Geographic*, April 22, 2014.
14 Suzana Herculano-Houzel, *The Human Advantage, A New Understanding of How Our Brain Became Remarkable*, *Proceedings of the National Academy of Sciences* (Boston: MIT Press, 2016), p. 187.
15 *Ibid.*
16 Delwen Samuel, Mark Nesbitt, "Approaches to the Archaeology of Food," *Petits Propos Culinaires 54*, 1996.
17 Jean-Lous Flandrin, Massimo Montanari, ed., *Food: A Culinary History* (New York: Columbia University Press, 2013), p. 39.
18 Caterina Pisu, "Trevignano Romano: Il Patrimonio Archaeologico," 26 March 2016. Pisu is scientific director of the Museo della Navigazione nelle Acque Interne at Capodimonte. Blog dedicated to Ofelio Maciucchi.
19 Ofelio Maciucchi, *Trevignano Romano, La Storia*, Comune di Trevignano, 1967, p. 11.
20 *Ibid.*
21 *Ibid.*

22 "Anguillara Sabazia," *Sabatino storia e storia dell'arte*, September 2017, www.lagosabatino.com.
23 Antonio Bazzarini, G. Pothier, *Le Pandette di Giustiniano*, Vol. 2, 1833, on Roman law in which he cites the *Epistulae* of Proculus.
24 Paolo Bondi da Fiumalbo, *Memorie storiche sulla citta Sabazia* (Florence: Calasanziana), 1836. For the full text see University of Illinois, https://archive.org/stream/memoriestoriches00bond_0/memoriestoriches00bond_0_djvu.txt.
25 Maciucchi, *op cit.*, p. 16.
26 Roberto Manigrasso, "Un'opera di drenaggio nel territorio di Trevignano Romano," Fast Online Documents & Research, Asso. Int. di Archeo Classica, Rome, See: http://www.fastionline.org/docs/FOLDER-it-2004-23.pdf.
27 Elena Felluca, *Aqua Traiana e Aqua Paula, un acquedotto lungo 2000 anni,* Vol. 4, Bracciano, 2017.
28 R. Taylor, G.Isidori, E. O'Neill, M. O'Neill, K. Rinne, "New Wine for Old Bottles: New Research on the Sources of the Aqua Traiana," *The Waters of Rome*, No. 9, Jan. 2016, p. 2.
29 *Ibid.*, p. 22
30 Franco Mezzetti, Ed., *Trevignano Romano,* (Trevignano: Collana Sabatina, 1969), p. 26.
31 Malcolm Bell, "An Imperial Flour Mill on the Janiculum" (Rome: Ecole Française Publication, 1994) p. 83.
32 Lucia Buonadonna, "Il lago di Bracciano e le 'mille once della discordia'", Associazione culturale Arca sul Lago. Buonadonna is archivist at Anguillara Sabazia.
33 Maciucchi, *op. cit.*, p. 130.
34 Deborah Needleman, "Who Will Save These Dying Italian Towns?", *The New York Times*, Sept. 7, 2017.
35 Lino Grifone, *Trevignano Romano,* (Trevignano: Collana Sabatina, 1969), p. 55.
36 T. Cecchini, E. Chinappi, C. D'Anna, *Guida al Castello di Bracciano e Dintorni* (Capranica: La Caravella Editrice, 2015), p. 43.
37 http://www.pbs.org/empires/medici/medici/murder.html.
38 Cecchini, *op. cit.*, p. 63.
39 Maciucchi, *op cit.*, p. 130.
40 Grifone, *op. cit.*, p. 55.
41 For many of these details about nineteenth-century life in Trevignano, I am grateful to M. S. Sorrenti Terlizzi and G. Bianchi Onori, Ed., *Trevignano Racconta*, a collection of brief essays by Trevignano citizens published by the Centro Sportivo e Culturale, Trevignano, 1980.
42 A. Morichelli, G. Pentassuglio, E. Trunzo, *Storia di famiglie, di donne e di uomini nella Trevignano dei secoli scorsi,* Archivi della Memoria (Ronciglione: BCC Credito Cooperativo Bank, 2015), p. 67.
43 Mary M. Voigt, "Hajji Firuz Tepe, Iran, the Neolithic Settlement", *Hasanlu*, Vol. I: (Philadelphia: University of Pennsylvania Museum Monograph), 1983
44 P. McGovern, D. Giusker, L. Exner, M. Voigt, "Neolithic resinated wine," *Scientific Correspondence* (Philadelphia: University of Pennsylvania, Nov. 2009). Prof. Patrick E. McGovern directs the university's Biomolecular Archaeology Project for Cuisine, Fermented Beverages and Health.
45 James Owen, "Earliest Known Winery Found in Armenian Cave," *National Geographic News*, Jan. 12, 2011.
46 Giampiero Castellotti, *Piazze in Piazza* (Rome: Spedizioni publishers, 2016), introduction by sociologist Giuseppe De Rita. The title translates as "Piazzas in the Piazza".
47 Stefano Ronchetti, *Hitnes a Trevignano Romano, Genesi di un murale* (Trevignano: Comune, 2018).
48 Frank Getlein, *Milton Hebald*, The Viking Press (New York: 1971), p. 12.
49 Luigia Cecchini, Aldo Lorenzini, *Come Parlavamo, Dai ricordi degli anziani trevignanesi,* from the series *La Memoria da Salvare* (Roma: Editore A. Spada, Banca di Credito Cooperativo, Formello andTrevignano Romano, 2006).

50 Corrado Giustiniani, *La Balilla di Nonno Fabio (*Rome: Fefè Editore, 2006).
51 Guido Aristarco, *Il Cinema Fascista, il prima e il dopo* (Bari: Edizioni Dedalo, 1996), p. 72.
52 Mezzetti, *op. cit.*
53 Mezzetti, *op. cit.*
54 Tridente, *op. cit.*
55 Maciucchi, *op. cit.*, p. 150.
56 Guido Ghini, ed., "Sulle Terre della Riforma: Luce sull'Italia agricola del dopoguerra", Arsial Comunicazione Istituzionale (Lazio Region: July 5, 2012).
57 Andrea Mariuzzo, "Land reform in the 1950s in Italy and the United States: The thinking of Mario Einaudi," *Modern Italy*, Vol. 18 Issue 4 (Cambridge: Jan. 2013), pp. 355-371.
58 S. H. Franklin, "Social Structure and Land Reform in Southern Italy," *Sociological Review*, November 1961, p. 323.
59 Maciucchi, *op. cit.*, p 147.
60 Paddy Agnew, "Bar saga mirrors 20th century Italy, from fascism to feminism," *The Irish Times*, July 4, 2011.
61 Elena Felluca, "Sabazia," *Lago Sabatino*, (undated), see: http://www.lagosabatino.com/sabazia. Felluca is the author of *Sabatia Regio, Studi, esplorazione e ricerche nel territorio del Lago di Bracciano*, Vols. I, II, III.
62 Maciucchi, *op. cit.*, p. 17.
63 www.ilsussidiario.net/News/Cronaca/2018/7/5/Veggente-Trevignano-Madonna-mi-ha-predetto-terremoto-di-Amatrice-Video-preghiamo-per-salvare-il-mondo-/829016/ July 5, 2018.
64 M. Azzella, C. Ricotta, C. Blasi, "Aquatic macrophyte diversity assessment," *Limnologica 43* (6), (Rome: Sapienza University, Dec. 2016).
65 Brian Maffly, "Great Salt Lake at near-record low," *The Salt Lake Tribune*, (Salt Lake City, Utah, Feb. 1, 2015).
66 www.brittanica.com/list/7-lakes-that-are-drying up.
67 *The Daily Telegraph* (London: April 5, 2010).
68 Shawn E. Carroll, "Ancient & Medieval Falconry: Origins & Functions in Medieval England," *The Crown & Helm*, January, May 1996, see http://www.r3.org/richard-iii/fifteenth-century-life/fifteenth-century-life-articles/ancient-medieval-falconry.
69 Giuseppe Tomassetti, *La Campagna Romana* (Rome: Banco di Roma, 1910).
70 Vivien Greene, editor, *Italian Futurism, 1909–1944: Reconstructing the Universe* (New York: Solomon R. Guggenheim Museum, 2014).
71 Steinar Aas, "New Perspectives on the Italia tragedy and Umberto Nobile," *Polar Research*, Vol. 24, 2005. Historian Aas of the University of Tromso, Norway, blames Amundsen's rivalry, and quotes Norwegian Communist newspaper calling exploration part of "imperialistic colonization policy" aimed at enhancing Italian imperialism.
72 Harvey M. Solomon, Philip Cala-Lazar, "The role of radio in rescuing the survivors of the airship Italia," Polar Research, Vol. 27, Issue 1. See: https://onlinelibrary.wiley.com/doi/full/10.1111/j.1751-8369.2008.00047.
73 Film Archiv Austria, ICT Ad Duas Lauros Rome, April 13, 2014, see: https://www.youtube.com/watch?v=98Rk0Evd7B4.
74 Massimo Mondini, *The Italian Air Force Museum of Vigna di Valle* (Rome: UTET, 2010), p. 14.

Bibliography

AAS, Steiner, "New Perspectives on the Italia tragedy and Umberto Nobile," Norway: *Polar Research*, , Vol. 24, 2005)

ARISTARCO, Guido, *Il Cinema Fascista, il prima e il dopo* (Bari: Edizioni Dedalo, 1996)

AZZELLA, M., Ricotta, C., Blasi, C., "Aquatic macrophyte diversity assessment," *Limnologica 43* (6), (Rome: Sapienza University, Dec. 2016)

BANDINELLI, Angela Carlino, *Parlando di Bracciano...* (Roma: Edizioni Mediterranee, 1989)

BAZZARINI, Antonio, G. Pothier, *Le Pandette di Giustiniano*, Vol 2, 1833

BELL, Malcolm, "An Imperial Flour Mill on the Janiculum" (Rome: Ecole Francaise Publication, 1994)

BIGAZZI, G., Radi, G., Odone, M., "The Italian Obsidian sources," (Hungary: *Archeometriai Muhely*, Jan. 2005)

BONDI DA FIUMALBO, Paolo, *Memorie storiche sulla città Sabozia ora lago Sabatino, sulla origine di Trevignano* (Florence: Calasanziana, 1836, in English at Saraswati Press, U.S., 2012)

BUONADONNA, Lucia, "Il lago di Bracciano e le 'mille once della discordia'" (Bracciano: published by the Associazione culturale Arca sul Lago), Sept. 2017

CARUSO, Ida, "Lake Bracciano: the historic landscape," *Trevignano Romano Museo Civico e Area Archaeologica*, Comune di Trevignano, 2002.

CARROLL, Shawn E., "Ancient & Medieval Falconry: Origins & Functions in Medieval England," *The Crown & Helm* (New York, London: Richard III Society, January, May 1996

CASTELLOTTI, Giampiero, *Piazze in Piazza* (Rome: Spedizioni publishers, 2016),

CECCHINI, Luigia, LORENZINI, Aldo, *Come Parlavamo, Dai ricordi degli anziani trevignanesi,* from the series *La Memoria da Salvare* (Roma: Editore A. Spada, con Banca di Credito Cooperativo, Formello e Trevignano Romano, 2006)

COTTRELL, Robert, *Roger Nash Baldwin and the American Civil Liberties Union* (New York: Columbia University Press, 2001)

DELWEN, Samuel, Mark Nesbitt, "Approaches to the Archaeology of Food," *Petits Propos Culinaires 54,* Ed., Alan Davidson, 1996)

FELLUCA, Elena, "Sabazia," *Lago Sabatino*, (undated, see: http://www.lagosabatino.com/sabazia/

FLANDRIN, Jean-Lous, Montanari, Massimo ed., *Food: A Culinary History* (New York: Columbia University Press, 2013)

FRANKLIN, S. H., "Social Structure and Land Reform in Southern Italy," (New York: *Sociological Review*, Vol. 9, Issue 3, November 1961)

GASPERINI, Lidio, "El tesoro de Vicarello, un gran descubrimiento arqueologica del siglo XIX," *Gerion, Revista de Historia Antiqua* Vol 26, (Madrid: No II, 2008)

GETLEIN, Frank, *Milton Hebald*, The Viking Press (New York: 1971),

GHINI, Guido, editor, "Sulle Terre della Riforma: Luce sull'Italia agricola del dopoguerra" (Rome: Arsial Comunicazione Istituzionale, July 5, 2012)

GIUFFRIDA, Salvatore, "Emergenze della capitale: Nella rete gruviera sparisce quasi la metà dell'acqua di Roma," (Rome: *La Repubblica*, June 20, 2017)

GIUSTINIANI, Corrado, *La Balilla di Nonno Fabio (*Rome: Fefè Editore, 2006)

GREENE, Vivien, Editor, *Italian Futurism, 1909–1944: Reconstructing the Universe* (New York: Solomon R. Guggenheim Museum, 2014)

GRIFONI, Lino, *Trevignano Romano* (Rome: Collana Sabatino, 1969)

MACIUCCHI, Ofelio, *Una Generazione Ricorda*, 1960-1980, Vol 1 and 2 (Trevignano Romano: Cassa Rurale e Artigiana di Trevignano, 1981, 1986)

MACIUCCHI, Ofelio, *Trevignano Romano, La Storia* (Trevignano Romano: Comune di Trevignano, 1967, 1997)

MAFFLY, Brian, "Great Salt Lake at near-record low," *The Salt Lake Tribune* (Salt Lake City, Utah, Feb. 1, 2015)

MANIGRASSO, Roberto, "Un'opera di drenaggio nel territorio di Trevignano Romano" (Rome: FastOnlineDocuments & Research, Associazione Internazionale di Archeologia Classica, 2004)

MARIUZZO, Andrea, *Land reform in the 1950s in Italy and the United States: the thinking of Mario Einaudi*, pp. 355-371

MCGOVERN, P., GIUSKER, D., EXNER, L., VOIGT, M., "Neolithic resinated wine," *Scientific Correspondence* (Philadelphia: University of Pennsylvania, Nov. 2009).

MEZZETTI, Franco, editor, *Trevignano Romano*, Collana Sabatina (Roma: Edizione Tevere), 1969

MONDINI, Massimo, *The Italian Air Force Museum of Vigna di Valle* (Rome: UTET, 2010)

MORICHELLI, A., PENTASSUGLIO, G., TRUNZO, E., *Storia di famiglie, di donne e di uomini nella Trevignano dei secoli scorsi*, Archivi della Memoria (Ronciglione, Viterbo: BCC Credito Cooperativo bank, 2015)

NIBBY, Antonio, *Analisi Storico-Topografico-Antiquaria della Carta de'Dintorni di Roma*, Vol. III (Campagna di Roma, 1837)

OWEN, James, "Earliest Known Winery Found in Armenian Cave," *National Geographic News*, Jan. 12, 2011

RONCHETTI, Stefano, *Hitnes a Trevignano Romano, Genesi di un murale* (Trevignano: Comune di Trevignano Romano, 2018)

ROSATI, F. Panvini, "Monete della stipe di Vicarello nel Museo Nazionale Romano," (Rome: *Pontifical Academy of Roman Archaeology*, XL, 1967-68)

RUPPI, Rebecca, "Prehistoric Dining: The Real Paleo Diet," *National Geographic*, April 22, 2014

SANTOCCHI, Augusto, *I Luoghi dell'Acqua nel Territorio di Bracciano*(Bracciano: Archivio Storico Comunale di Bracciano, 2010)

SAUNDERS, Nicholas J. *The Poppy: A History of Conflict, Loss, Remembrance, and Redemption* (London: Oneworld Publications, 2013)

SOLOMON, Harvey M., Cala-Lazar, Philip, "The role of radio in rescuing the survivors of the airship Italia" (Norway: *Polar Research*, Vol. 27, Issue 1, 2008)

SORRENTI TERLIZZI, M. S., BIANCHI ONORI, G., Editors, *Trevignano Racconta* (Trevignano Romano: Centro Sportivo e Culturale, 1980)

TALEB, Nassim Nicholas, *The Black Swan* (New York: Random House, 2007; London: Penguin, 2010)

TAYLOR, R., Isidori, G., O'Neill, E., O'Neill, M., Rinne, K., "New Wine for Old Bottles: New Research on the Sources of the Aqua Traiana," *The Waters of Rome*, No. 9 (Virginia: Jan. 2016)

THOMSON DE GRUMMOND, Nancy, *Etruscan Myth, Sacret History, and Legend*. (Philadelphia: University of Pennsylvania Museum of Archaeology, 2006).

TINÈ,Vincenzo, "Il Neolitico in Italia," http://www.mundusonline.it/PDF/75.pdf

TOMASSETTI, Giuseppe, *La Campagna Romana* (Rome: Banco di Roma, 1910)

TRIDENTE, Pasquale, *Trevignano Ieri ed Oggi* (Comune di Trevignano, 2010)

VOIGT, Mary M., "Hajji Firuz Tepe, Iran, the Neolithic Settlement", *Hasanlu*, Vol. I: (Philadelphia: University of Pennsylvania Museum Monograph), 1983